LIFE AT THE DAWN OF THE 20TH CENTURY

LIFE AT THE DAWN OF THE 20TH CENTURY

Reader's Digest

Published by
THE READER'S DIGEST ASSOCIATION LIMITED
London   New York   Sydney
Montreal   Cape Town

LAZY DAYS A boating trip on the River Thames at Henley in the early 1900s epitomises the elegance and leisured grace of middle-class England. Inset: Large-scale immigration to the cities led to urban overcrowding, as in New York's Lower East Side.

LIFE AT THE DAWN OF THE 20TH CENTURY
Edited and designed by Toucan Books Limited
Sole author: James Cochrane

First edition copyright © 1996
The Reader's Digest Association Limited
Berkeley Square House, Berkeley Square,
London W1X 6AB

Copyright © 1996
Reader's Digest Association Far East Limited
Philippines copyright © 1996
Reader's Digest Association Far East Limited
All rights reserved

Printing and binding: Printer Industria Gráfica S.A., Barcelona
Separations: Rodney Howe Limited, London
Paper: Perigord-Condat, France

ISBN 0 276 42134 5

Front cover (clockwise from top right): Dunce in cap, *c*.1900; English tea party, 1910; Marie Curie, 1917; Labour cycling club, Yarmouth, 1906; health manual, *c*.1900; French aviation poster.

Back cover (clockwise from top left): Paris métro; typewriter, *c*.1900; French miners; women in garden, *c*.1906; US postcard announcing new baby; card on motor racing, Germany, *c*.1903; couple dancing.

Page 1: EDWARDIAN SUMMER Shrimping at Scarborough, England, in the last summer before the Great War.

Pages 2-3: AMERICAN DREAM A family having a picnic beside their Model T Ford in 1915.

HEALTH AND SAFETY A Red Cross nurse symbolises a new concern for public health and hygiene.

HOME COMFORTS The interior of a German middle-class home in 1907.

CONTENTS

TIME OF THEIR LIVES For the children of the well-to-do, the 1890s and early 1900s were a Golden Age.

JOIE DE VIVRE
An advertisement of the 1890s captures a gaiety that was peculiarly French.

DANCING GIRLS The Sisters Levey, with their Ostrich Dance, reflect a new frivolity of taste.

CAR CRAZY By 1913 Americans had taken enthusiastically to the motor car.

CHANGE IN THE AIR

The years around the dawn of the 20th century were a time of ostentatious

wealth, middle-class prosperity and appalling poverty, of splendour and misery,

of conservatism and invention, and of security and anxiety.

AFTER THE catastrophe of the First World War, people from the middle and upper classes in Europe and North America – and in countries such as Australia and New Zealand, too – looked back to the years between 1890 and 1914 as a kind of golden age of peace and plenty. The French called those years *la belle époque*; the British thought of them as the Edwardian Era (although King Edward VII had reigned only from 1901 to 1910); and the German writer Stefan Zweig called them the 'Age of Golden Security' and 'a sweet time to be alive'.

Memories of those years were perhaps influenced by the fact that the weather in the summer of 1914, when the Great War began, was unusually fine, but there is no doubt that for those who were rich, or even comfortably off, the two decades before 1914 were a period of unparalleled leisure and luxury, when science and technology seemed only to be adding to the conveniences of life and the possibilities of passing it agreeably.

Above all, this was the last period in which there was a large and secure leisured class. Living on the rents from land or the returns from investments – at a period when prices were stable and inflation almost unheard of – were a large number of people who did not need to work for a living and would have thought it vulgar to do so. This leisured class produced many of the writers, artists and thinkers of the day, and many of its members devoted themselves to charitable activities. Nevertheless, for the majority of the rich, everyday life was a matter of filling the time delightfully and attending to the rituals of High Society. In his recollections of the summer of 1896, Maurice Baring, from a wealthy English banking family, captures much of what people remembered as the magical charm of the time: 'I went to the Derby that year and backed Persimmon; to the first performance of Mrs Campbell's *Magda* the same night; I saw Duse at

A LEISURED CLASS Spectators enjoy Cowes Regatta, an important annual event in the lives of the Edwardian upper class.

Drury Lane and Sarah Bernhardt at Daly's; I went to Ascot; I went to balls; I stayed at Panshanger; and at Wrest, at the end of summer, where a constellation of beauty moved in muslin and straw hats and yellow roses on the lawns of gardens designed by Le Notre, delicious with ripe peaches on old brick walls, with the smell of verbena and sweet geranium; and stately with large avenues, artificial lakes and white temples; and we bicycled in the warm night past ghostly cornfields by the light of a large full moon.'

But it was not just the very rich who could look back to those days with pleasant memories. The British economist J.M. Keynes, writing in 1920, recalled the days when: 'The inhabitant of London could order by telephone, sipping his morning tea in bed, the various products of the whole earth in such quantity as he might see fit, and reasonably expect their early delivery on his doorstep, ... [and could] ... secure forthwith, if he wished it, cheap and

A NEW INDUSTRIAL REVOLUTION   Germany led the world in making high-quality steel, as in this Krupp steel plant.

comfortable means of transit to any country or climate, without passport or other formality, could dispatch his servant to the neighbouring office of a bank for such supply of the precious metals as might seem convenient, and could then proceed abroad to foreign quarters without knowledge of their religion, language or customs, having coined wealth upon his person, and would consider himself greatly aggrieved and much surprised at the least interference. But, most important of all, he regarded this state of affairs as normal, certain and permanent, except in the direction of further improvements, and any deviation from it as aberrant, scandalous and avoidable.'

Although domestic telephones were still rare in the early 1900s, such a lifestyle – with servants,

tradesmen anxious to please, a growing range of manufactured goods to buy, and rapid, safe and comfortable transport by motor car, train or ship across a world at peace – was enjoyed by large numbers of people in the 1890s and early 1900s.

FILL-UP   An American gasoline seller supplies fuel to motorists.

8

DREADNOUGHT In the early 1900s
Germany and Britain competed
with one another to build giant
warships such as the *Bismarck.*

The picture of long, sunny afternoons in English country houses, of elegant men and women relaxing in the outdoor cafés of Paris or Berlin, of tranquil villages and prosperous towns, is a true, but also of course a partial one. Although the standard of living of working people, especially in the United States, had improved in the last decades of the 19th century, perhaps as many as one-third of the population lived at or below the poverty line, in overcrowded, insanitary housing, with such concomitants of poverty as poor health, drunkenness and high infant mortality. The gulf between rich and poor had perhaps never been so wide or so deep, for the growth of commerce and industry in the latter part of the 19th century had produced enormous new fortunes, and wealth was being displayed with an ostentation that many observers at the time thought tasteless and shocking.

Nor was the world entirely at peace. Britain went to war with the Boers in South Africa and suffered humiliating defeats. Throughout the early 1900s there were fears of a European war, as Britain and Germany engaged in a costly and dangerous 'Dreadnought race', competing with each other to build giant battleships, and the foundries of Europe piled up more and more massive and deadly weapons. The newly industrialised Japan had defeated Russia in war and shaken confidence in European invincibility.

Industrialisation had created a self-conscious urban working class, some of whom were determined to force a more equitable distribution of wealth. Socialist parties were formed in all the industrialised countries of the world in the early 1900s, some of them with a programme of violent revolution inspired by the teachings of Karl Marx. In Britain and Germany, workers were joining trade unions in their millions. Strikes, sometimes violent, were frequent. Anarchists, committed to the violent overthrow of the present form of society, threw bombs in the capitals of Europe. Suffragettes tied themselves to railings or went on hunger strike in a campaign to win the vote for women, denied to them almost everywhere. Revolution exploded in Russia in 1905, creating fears of similar revolutions elsewhere.

THE OLD WORLD AND THE NEW

Some historians have suggested that the 19th century really came to an end in 1914, but everywhere in the early 1900s there were signs of a new world existing side by side with the old. The United States was already the world's richest nation. Income there was 25 per cent higher than the average income in Britain and five times the average in continental Europe. By 1913, America's manufacturing output was equal to that of Britain, Germany and France combined. In political institutions, in manners and fashions, and in the manufacture and supply of consumer goods, the United States was by far and away the most 'modern' of countries.

By contrast, one did not have to travel far in

NEW WOMAN Some
feminists in the 1890s
affected a masculine
style of dress.

PARIS IN 1900 The Grand Palais was built to celebrate the birth of the 20th century.

Europe to find manners and customs and costumes that were still almost medieval in character, not least in its imperial courts, in its universities and among its traditional peasantries. This was still a world in which men tilled the soil in immemorial ways, in which craftsmen were apprenticed to ancient skills, in which upper and lower classes often behaved towards each other like two separate human species.

France, the United States and Britain had democratic government, but even in Britain the government was largely chosen from the traditional ruling class; and in Germany and in the Austro-Hungarian Empire, the monarch and the ministers he appointed still had very real power, especially over matters of defence and the conduct of foreign relations. The civilian governments of the democracies could be contrasted with the gorgeously uniformed courts of the European empires with their plumed helmets, laced uniforms and polished riding boots. Vienna was still a city of magnificent imperial balls, danced to the music of Strauss. Russia was still in many ways ruled like a medieval kingdom, in which every rank in the civil service had its own uniform, and a monk, Grigory Rasputin, could exercise enormous power through his influence on the Empress.

In most of the democracies, the suffrage was limited to adult males; only in Finland, Norway, New Zealand, Australia and the State of Wyoming did women have the vote before 1914. A small minority of women were reacting to this fact with

CROWD-MOVER One of the features of the Paris Exposition of 1889 was this moving platform – the first ever produced – which conveyed visitors around the site.

GROUND-TO-AIR
The development of the motor car engine led within a very few years to powered flight.

passion, sometimes even with violence; others were breaking into the professions, hitherto exclusively male, and into the universities; and thousands were finding employment outside the home for the first time, as elementary schoolteachers.

The massive shift towards industrialisation, and the shift of population from countryside to town, that had taken place in Britain early in the 19th century, now began to happen in western Europe, and especially in Germany and the Netherlands; even in France the percentage of the population that was employed on the land had fallen below 50 per cent by 1900; in Britain it was below 10 per cent, by far the lowest in the world. Even Russia, with its many millions of peasants not long released from serfdom, was industrialising

THE RISE OF THE TELEPHONE

IN MARCH 1876, Alexander Graham Bell transmitted the first words by telephone to his partner, Thomas Watson: 'Mr Watson, come here, I want you.' At the time, Watson could not reply, for Bell's new telephone was still a one-way instrument.

In the early years, the telephone was seen as a medium of entertainment rather than of communication. William Orton, President of

EARLY CALL
A telephone user in the 1880s tries out the new instrument.

Western Union, turned down an offer to buy the patent outright for $100 000, saying, 'What use would this company make of an electrical toy?' British Post Office officials, meanwhile, questioned its usefulness in a country where there was an abundance of domestic servants and errand boys. At the Paris Exhibition of 1881 people queued to hear music transmitted by telephone, and there were 'theatrephones' in the Paris boulevards, linked to local theatres.

After Thomas Edison had improved the telephone transmitter, Americans began to change their minds. By 1881 there were 132 692 telephones in use in the United States compared with only 6 in 1877, and most of the larger American cities had a telephone exchange. It was the development of the telephone exchange, and of

a telephone number system, that transformed it into a medium of communication. By 1894 there were over 250 000 telephones in the United States, and their use had spread to rural areas.

In Britain the first telephone exchange was opened in London in 1879 and the first list of subscribers was printed in 1880; London had a telephone link with Birmingham in 1890 and with Paris the following year.

Yet in London in 1881, there was only one telephone for every 3000 people, compared with one for every 200 people in Chicago; the postmaster general declared that while 'gas and water were necessities for every inhabitant, telephones were not and never would be'. By 1900 there were still only 210 000 telephones in the whole of Britain.

ABSOLUTE MONARCH Nicholas II is crowned Tsar and Autocrat of all the Russias in 1895.

rapidly. Everywhere in the industrialising parts of Europe, cities were growing at an astonishing rate, and were also being transformed by modern transportation systems.

RICH AND POOR

In the advanced industrial countries such as Britain and the United States, overall wealth greatly increased during the decades before the First World War. In Britain in 1870 the average income had been 25 per cent above the level needed for bare subsistence; by 1914 it was a comfortable 150 per cent, enabling large numbers of people to furnish and decorate their homes, buy new clothes and enjoy their leisure. But in all the countries of the Western world, there were great inequalities of wealth. In Britain, for example, the richest 2 per cent of the population had assets worth almost three

times as much as all the rest of the population put together; in the year 1914, 4 per cent of the population owned 90 per cent of all the wealth bequeathed. In Europe, 30 per cent of people lived below the official poverty line, while in the United States 40 per cent of wage-earning families lived below the poverty line in slums as terrible as any to be seen in Europe.

The creation of a large industrial working class actually made class differences more marked than before. Millions still worked as before as craftsmen or artisans in countless different skilled trades run as small family businesses. But for the millions of new waged factory workers, there was a sharp distinction between skilled and unskilled. Roughly 75 per cent of Britain's population – and rather less in other European countries – could be described as manual workers and their dependants. Their

SOCIAL UNREST Workers demonstrate in London's Trafalgar Square in February 1914 and (right) miners go on strike in France in 1906. Such events led to fears of violent revolution.

annual incomes could vary widely, and crucially, from as much as £200 for skilled workers to below the subsistence level: from a state of modest prosperity down to a level of near-destitution. In addition, the very poor were actually paying more for their food than the better-off because, with their minute incomes, they were obliged to buy goods in disproportionately priced 'penny packets'.

These great differences in wealth did not go unnoticed. As industrial workers increasingly came together in large factories and urban areas, there was a growing class consciousness. There were whole towns or city areas, such as Wedding in Berlin or some of the East End boroughs of London, where the population consisted almost entirely of manual workers and their families, something quite new in collective human experience.

Discontent inevitably grew, and some of the more enlightened governments, for example in Germany and Britain, began to try to anticipate it by introducing basic labour and welfare legislation. In such countries, the state began to intervene in matters of factory conditions, hours of work and

basic health provision. Old-age pensions were introduced in Germany in the late 1880s, and in Britain in 1909, along with modest forms of unemployment and health insurance. In the United States, on the other hand, all such state-inspired welfare reforms were resisted; not even child labour was controlled by Federal law. Instead, progressive American companies began to introduce their own welfare programmes, including schemes for cheap workers' housing.

Everywhere, but perhaps especially in Britain, the working class clung to its own cultural identity. Working-class people wore caps and mufflers and lived close together in terraced housing; they followed their own sports such as football, pigeon-fancying and dog-racing and had their own pubs

DYNASTIC MARRIAGE Consuela Vanderbilt's marriage to the Duke of Marlborough was typical of many alliances between American wealth and European rank.

Above them was a large middle class of professionals, businessmen and 'rentiers' (whose unearned income came from investments and rents), who enjoyed growing prosperity and were able to keep up substantial houses with several servants. They were also able to purchase an increasing number of services and consumer goods, especially in the United States, where there were already the beginnings of a 'Consumer Revolution'.

Among the middle class, incomes varied greatly. A successful lawyer might earn £25 000 per annum, compared with a master in a private school earning perhaps £200-£300. For purposes of comparison, a teacher in an elementary school earned less than £100 per annum and domestic servants earned between £10 and £30, plus their food and lodging. An income of £1000 per annum (roughly £50 000 in today's values) was regarded as the level at which one could be truly 'comfortable'. It was at this level of income that one could enjoy a middle-class lifestyle, characterised by abundant spare time, the

and cafés. Socially above the level of the working class, a large lower-middle class consisted of small shopkeepers and self-employed artisans but also of growing numbers of waged white-collar workers.

HOLIDAY TRAVEL Londoners crowd Waterloo Station in May 1912 on their way to the seaside. The railways made travel possible for many people for the first time.

enjoyment of a range of goods and services, travel, and education beyond the elementary level.

At the top of the social pyramid were the rich and the very rich. Here, a distinction was still made between Old Money derived from land and the vast new fortunes made in commerce, manufacturing and finance, although Old and New Money were beginning to mingle. In Britain in particular, where land values had fallen sharply due to Free Trade, aristocrats replenished their fortunes by marrying into New Money and by taking an increasing interest in stocks and shares. The new rich acquired titles themselves – sometimes quite literally buying them from the government of the day.

The fabulously wealthy of the day, however, were the American millionaires – the Vanderbilts, Astors and others – who built their palaces on the avenues of Manhattan and their 40-bedroomed 'cottages' on Long Island. The daughters of American millionaires flocked across the Atlantic to marry blue blood, and the titled and landed bachelors of Britain and Europe responded, causing considerable resentment among the mothers of well-born English daughters. In 1896 the American heiress Consuela Vanderbilt married the 9th Duke of Marlborough (unhappily as it turned out), bringing a dowry of £2 million, and the railway heiress Helena Zimmerman became Duchess of Manchester.

A TIME OF CHANGE

The sense of stability and permanence in the years before the First World War was largely illusory. A man and woman who

HOMELESS **The slums of Paris were dismantled around the inhabitants to make way for new buildings.**

reached the age of 30 in 1914, living in a European or North American city, would probably have agreed that they had experienced more change in their lives than had been seen in the entire history of the world. They would have been right. Their city itself would have grown and changed almost beyond recognition. The motor car, an invention of the 1890s, was a common sight by 1914, when much public transport and commercial traffic was also motorised. In the United States, the Model T Ford had even brought motoring within the means of ordinary people. Aeroplanes, which had flown for the first time at the beginning of the 20th century (the first powered flight was by Orville and Wilbur Wright in 1903), were developed enough only a few years later to play their part in the Great War.

Telephones and typewriters were transforming business. Cities were beginning to be lit by electricity. The cinema, after only 20 years, was a familiar part of everyday life, already producing 'film stars' with international reputations. People could buy gramophone records, and were dancing in a manner, and to sounds and rhythms, unheard of

STREET PARTY **London's East Enders celebrate the coronation of King George V in 1910.**

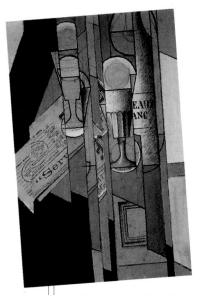

MODERNISM The ideas of modern art, as expressed in the work of the Cubist painter Juan Gris and the Futurist sculptures of Umberto Boccioni, were established before the First World War.

before 1890. Attitudes and values were changing too. High Victorian ideas about morality and duty were beginning to give way, at least among the young and the well-to-do, to the notion that life was there to be enjoyed. Religion was losing its authority, and many, especially among intellectuals and among the urban working class, were discarding it altogether. The State was beginning to intervene in people's lives, providing education and basic welfare, setting limits on working hours, and legislating on matters that would have been unheard of earlier in the 19th century.

Under the surface, still deeper changes were taking place. In the early 1900s, Picasso and Braque had already created Cubism and set the style for the art of the 20th century; Schoenberg had established the principles of modern atonal music; Stravinsky had created a riot in the Theatre des Champs-Elysées with his radical new ballet, *The Rite of Spring*, in 1913; the theory of modernist functional architecture was in place and some modernist buildings had already been constructed before 1914; Einstein had published his Special Theory of Relativity and Max Planck his quantum theory; Freud was at work in Vienna and had founded psychoanalysis.

Only a few people were aware of these developments, which were to shape our own lives in so many ways, but at the birth of the new century there was a feeling of change in the air. When crowds gathered in Trafalgar Square, in Times Square, in the Place de la Concorde or on Unter den Linden at midnight on December 31, 1900, to greet the New Year, they believed they were at the beginning of an exciting new era, not at the end of an old one.

In many ways, the period before the First World War anticipated the concerns of our own age – with changes in the structure of family life, the rise of feminism, the labour movement, modernism in the arts, the growth of moral and religious uncertainty, and the emergence of modern science and technology. Yet in other respects – with its imperial monarchies, its dominant leisured class, its familiarity with endemic disease, grinding poverty and high infant mortality, and its essential confidence in the permanence of Empire and of European civilisation in general – the world of 1914 was swept away for ever by the cataclysm of the Great War.

THE GUNS OF AUGUST French reservists report for duty after the declaration of war in August 1914.

Town and Country

Cities grew larger, buildings grew taller and public transport systems

transformed urban life. Industrialisation produced a self-conscious

working class and social discontent grew, threatening revolution.

The railway and motor car linked town and country as never before.

The countryside was changing more slowly, but agriculture was

becoming more efficient and more mechanised.

TOWNS AND TRANSPORT

At the dawn of the 20th century, the cities of Europe and North America

were expanding rapidly and city life was undergoing great change with

the development of public transport systems.

THE DRAMATIC growth that had taken place in Britain's major cities and towns earlier in the 19th century was happening elsewhere in Europe and in North America by the end of the century. The population of Greater London was now 7 million, but by 1914, 51 cities in continental Europe and 20 in the USA had over 250 000 inhabitants – a size achieved by only a handful before 1890.

The rapid growth of urban populations in Europe was particularly marked in German cities such as Essen, Hamburg, Dusseldorf, Nuremberg, Frankfurt-am-Main, Stuttgart, Leipzig, Dresden, Bremen and Hanover. In Holland, Rotterdam quadrupled in size between 1890 and 1910. This growth was due largely to rapid industrialisation – iron and steel, engineering, coal and shipbuilding. In the United States, Detroit's population swelled because of automobile manufacture; Cleveland's because of oil processing; and Chicago's because of meat packing, grain and lumber distribution, and steel-making. New York City expanded as a port and major commercial and financial centre, but also because of the rapid growth in a wide range of manufactures produced there, for example in the garment industry.

As the cities grew, they also changed in character. As business grew bigger and more complex, there was a demand for more and bigger commercial buildings. Earlier in the 19th century

TOWN TRAFFIC **Motorised and horse-drawn vehicles jostle and negotiate round each other at London's Charing Cross in 1912.**

most offices were essentially converted houses, and until the 1850s few commercial buildings were more than four or five stories high. By 1900, the relatively modest terraces of the mid 19th century had given way to massive purpose-built commercial buildings, department stores, hotels and apartment buildings.

The first safe electric elevator was installed in the Demarest Building in New York in 1859. Elevators meant that buildings could grow taller, and in New York and Chicago especially, they did so, thanks also to the use of the internal iron frame of columns and beams that carried the masonry walls. In addition, New York's granite bedrock meant that there was no need for complicated foundations for these high buildings. The skyscraper was born in the late 1860s; by the early 1900s it had created townscapes in those cities unlike anything to be seen elsewhere in the world.

TRAVELLING ABOUT TOWN

The shape of cities was also changed by more efficient public transport in the form of local railway systems, trolleys and tramcars. Local railways were steam-driven, but from the 1880s

SKYSCRAPER **The Fuller Building, known as the Flat-Iron, was New York's earliest skyscraper. Tall buildings were constructed on iron frames, as in the *Morning Post* building (inset) in the Strand, London.**

TICKETS, PLEASE Tickets for travel on the London transport system. The system gave people easy access to the city and the surrounding countryside.

London in 1911. By that time, too, motorised transport was firmly established. Motor buses, independent of both rails and wires, began to appear in London in the early 1900s, and by 1914 motorised lorries were competing strongly with horse-drawn goods carriages.

Cities solved their transport problems in other ways as well, for example by building elevated railways, as in New York and Berlin, or by going underground: London opened its first electrically powered 'tube' in 1900, to be followed by Glasgow, Berlin, Paris, Budapest and Hamburg. The first New York subway opened in 1904.

Trains, trolleys and trams changed the shape of cities. People were troubled at first by unsightly overhead electric wires or by having their streets dug up for the laying of tramlines, but there were clear benefits from the provision of rapid and cheap public transport. People could live farther from their places of work, and residential development could spread outwards from the industrial and commercial centre. The English word 'suburbia' was first coined in the 1890s to describe the kind of house-and-

onwards, electric tramways and trolleys became more common, with the United States and Germany in the lead. The first experimental electric tramway was established in Lichterfelde, a suburb of Berlin, in 1881. Britain as a whole was slower than continental Europe to adopt electric transport systems, but Glasgow pioneered electric tramways in the 1890s, running them municipally in a system that was widely followed. By 1914 tramways were commonplace; there were 2500 miles (4000 km) of tramway in the UK alone, and horse-drawn omnibuses were withdrawn from

METRO The Paris underground railway system was under construction in 1899, and (left) the ticket office at Gare St Lazare provided sumptuous surroundings for underground travellers, befitting the novel form of transport.

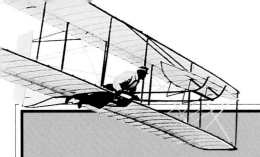

THE WRIGHT BROTHERS TAKE OFF

BIRD'S EYE VIEW One of the Wright brothers' earliest flying machines takes off.

WITH THE development of the motor-car engine, powered flight became a realistic goal. The race was on between the French, who were working hard on it, and two American bicycle-makers, Wilbur and Orville Wright, who were experimenting with gliders in Dayton, Ohio.

It was the Wright brothers' mastery of gliders that led to America's gift to Europe of powered flight. By 1903 they were making short experimental flights of 20 minutes at a height of 300 ft (90 m), using borrowed engines at first, but later their own. Nervous about patents, they worked in secret. Rumours of their achievements were received sceptically in Europe, where all kinds of flying machines had been built, but none of which had managed more than a short 'hop' of less than one minute's duration.

Then, in 1908, the Wright brothers made their first public flights. Wilbur flew at Le Mans in France in August that year; then Orville at Fort Meyer, Virginia, in September. Observers at Le Mans saw Wilbur take off, fly, bank, circle and return to his point of departure, using ailerons, movable flaps on the wings, to control the plane – a development that French designers had not produced. Between August and December that year he made more than 100 flights in France, 60 of them with passengers, and one of them lasting two and a half hours.

In 1909, Orville Wright made a series of demonstration flights from Tempelhof field in Berlin, and the German Kaiser made an enthusiastic speech about the military possibilities of the new invention.

garden lifestyle that was now possible for many, thanks to rail links with the city centre. By the early 1900s, commuting to and from the major cities was a familiar activity for many people.

Other forms of transport were also changing the possibilities of everyday life at the dawn of the 20th century. The bicycle reached something very like its modern form and was hugely popular among all classes. It gave working-class people a mobility they had never enjoyed before, and gave young men and women the opportunity to enjoy each other's company without the supervision of a chaperone.

For 1000 years, one of the great social divisions had been the one that existed between those who rode and those who walked. The bicycle, on the other hand, was a social equaliser. Along with the clothes designed for bicycling, it became one of the symbols of the era. Another was the transatlantic liner, now designed like a vast floating luxury hotel, fast and comfortable and apparently safe. The sinking of one of the supreme liners, the *Titanic*, in 1912, sent shock waves around the world and was seen by many as divine retribution for the materialism and complacency of the age.

Yet another symbol of the age was the aeroplane. When Orville and Wilbur Wright made the first powered flight in 1903, it seemed that the 20th century had truly been born. In 1908, the year in which Wilbur Wright impressed a sceptical European audience with his flight at Le Mans, aviation made real progress in Europe as well, and by the end of the year two French pilots, Henri Farman and Louis Bleriot, had
continued on page 24

ON TRACK
A tramcar in
Dunfermline,
Scotland, 1900.

THE RISE OF THE MOTOR CAR

THE PRINCIPAL inventor of the internal combustion engine for propelling vehicles was a German, Gottfried Daimler, who patented his engine in France in 1885. The Daimler company's own Mercedes series, unveiled in 1901, was to outstrip all competitors, but in the last years of the 19th century it was France that led the way in the development of the motor car, organising races, automobile clubs and annual car shows.

HORSELESS CARRIAGE The first Rolls-Royce appeared in 1903.

Britain lagged behind at first because of laws, designed for steam traction engines, that set a speed limit of 4 mph (6.4 km/h) and required a man with a red flag to walk in front. The change in this law in 1896 was celebrated by a motor-car test run from London to Brighton, still commemorated annually.

A branch of the Daimler company was established in Britain, but British manufacturers, several of them already established as bicycle-makers, were soon producing their own cars; they included names still familiar decades later, such as Singer, Humber, Rover, Morris, Vauxhall, Wolseley, Austin and, of course, Rolls-Royce. By 1914 there were 132 000 registered private cars in Britain, the highest number in Europe.

Development of the motor car in the United States was also slow at first, partly because of the absence of metalled roads between cities, but it took off rapidly in the 1900s. Whereas in Europe the car was still mainly a leisure vehicle for the well-to-do, its utilitarian value was rapidly recognised in North America, where popular ownership became

THE JOYS OF MOTORING An early motor car in the streets of Paris resembles a carriage on wheels, and (inset) a family enjoy an outing in a Fiat in the 1900s.

a reality decades earlier than in the Old World. By 1910 there were 200 American manufacturers, producing around 200 000 cars annually.

Henry Ford, who had built his first car in the last years of the 19th century, formed the Ford Motor Company in June 1903 and put on sale his Model A car for $850. His Model T, produced in large numbers from 1908, was adapted for use on country roads and was well within the means of ordinary people; by 1913 its price had fallen to $500. It was a serviceable vehicle, assembled on a moving assembly line from standardised parts, and was available only in black. It was particularly popular in rural communities, which it transformed, and it continued to be produced until 1927.

Ford's assembly-line manufacturing method, which was eventually to produce cars at the rate of 2000 a day, was imitated not only by other car manufacturers but in a wide range of other industries as well.

RACING DEMONS Within a few years of the invention of the motor car, it was being raced in competitions in the United States and drivers were hailed as conquering heroes, while a Michelin tyre advertisement (inset) extols the car's speed compared to more established forms of travel. More sedate was the family Ford (left), seen here with Henry Ford himself and his son Edsel in the front seats.

made flights of 20 minutes and 11 minutes respectively. In July 1909, Louis Bleriot made the first flight across the English Channel, in 37 minutes. However, for all the enthusiasm of the crowds and the daring exploits of the pilots at race meetings and aerial circuses, few recognised the aeroplane's potential, for both peacetime and wartime use.

PUBLIC UTILITIES

Another change that took place in the towns and cities of the time was the great increase in the provision of public services by municipal governments. The operation by local government of police and fire brigades and gas, water and sewage services – known in Britain as 'gas and water socialism' – was common everywhere, but German municipal authorities, in particular, went much further. The city of Düsseldorf, for example, operated the street railways, the slaughterhouses, public baths, public markets, hospitals, banks, a pawnshop and a cemetery, as well as supporting amenities such as libraries and museums, an art gallery, a theatre and a concert orchestra.

Germany also led the way in the new policy of zoning cities into separate industrial and residential areas, and Britain and Germany took that idea even further with the notion of the 'garden city', a city designed from the outset with

ARM OF THE LAW   A Paris policeman in the 1900s. The influence of the state was growing . . .

careful zoning and with plentiful open space, grass and trees. This idea had been pioneered by Ebenezer Howard, whose *Garden Cities of Tomorrow* was first published in 1898, and was actually realised at Letchworth, at Port Sunlight near Liverpool, at Bournville near Birmingham, at Hellerau near Dresden and in similar projects in Munich, Karlsruhe, Nuremberg and Frankfurt.

CITY BUILDINGS

At the beginning of the 20th century, most new buildings still reflected a variety of historical styles. A rough convention of the time was that churches were built in Gothic or Romanesque style, banks in classical style, and other large public buildings in Baroque. Nevertheless, a variety of period styles, or combinations of them, were still fashionable: French or Italian Renaissance, Dutch, 'Tudor', 'Queen Anne', even Egyptian and Babylonian. The new skyscrapers of New York and Chicago, although built on iron frames, carried decorative motifs from much earlier eras: the Graham Buildings (1898) in New York followed the style of the classical Greek column; the Metropolitan Life Building (New York, 1909) imitated the campanile in Venice; and the Woolworth Building (New York, 1913) was built in the Gothic style. The aim was for buildings to be opulent; however, they were often merely grandiose.

In the 1890s and early 1900s, other influences were at work. In England, the passionately argued views of William Morris and the Arts and Crafts Movement, with its commitment to simplicity, quality of materials and respect for craftsmanship, resulted in buildings and interiors that were both

AT YOUR SERVICE . . . and municipalities were providing increased public services, such as this French fire brigade.

SHOWN BY THE ELECTRIC SUPPLY

BRIGHTER LIVES An advertisement glamorises the very real difference that electricity made to people's lives. Right: Just as important in their own way were municipal refuse-collection services.

graceful and dignified, including some of the best country houses built during the period. Under Morris's influence, 'fine art' craftsmen produced a range of handcrafted furniture, textiles, wallpaper and metalwork.

In Europe generally, there was the much more powerful influence of Art Nouveau, known in Germany as Jügendstil and in Italy as Stile Liberty (after the London department store of that name, which exported Art Nouveau fabrics). Art Nouveau, with which the Arts and Crafts Movement became identified, was an attempt to create an entirely new decorative manner, free from references to the styles of the past, based on organic forms and eschewing the straight line in favour of asymmetrical curves wherever possible.

In architectural terms, it produced thousands of buildings throughout continental Europe; it can be seen in countless private houses in Belgium, in the stations of the Paris Metro, in the work of Antonio Gaudi in Barcelona, many of whose buildings resembled irregular, natural forms, and of the American architect Louis Henry Sullivan, who used Art Nouveau ironwork to decorate otherwise conventional buildings. On a smaller scale, it produced Tiffany lamps and the decorative

RUBBISH!

It was Eugene Poubelle, Prefect of Paris, who introduced the metal dustbin with a lid, still called a poubelle in France. At first this infuriated Paris rag-and-bone dealers, who were accustomed to picking rubbish from the gutters, but they were soon allowed by the authorities to raid the dustbins, provided that they exhibited their wares away from the centre of the city. This led to the founding of Paris's famous Marché aux Puces or flea market on the northern edge of the city.

glassware of René Lalique. Although Art Nouveau developed first in England, and although one of its major exponents was the Scottish architect and designer Charles Rennie Mackintosh, it was less influential on British than on Continental architecture. Nevertheless, even in Britain, it was high fashion for textile, jewellery and furniture design from 1890 to 1910.

FUNCTIONALISM

Art Nouveau died away rapidly after 1910. It was a style that depended heavily on skilled manual craftsmanship and was therefore expensive to execute. What the age really needed was a style that lent itself to machine construction. The future could already be seen in the structures, such as bridges and railway stations, that were being erected by civil engineers and industrial designers. Influenced by these functional structures, architects such as Frank Lloyd Wright in the United States, Otto Wagner in Vienna and Peter Behrens in Germany were beginning to condemn ornamentation in architecture and were calling for

PUT ANOTHER NICKEL IN

Flat, 7 in (18 cm) gramophone records began to appear in the 1890s; in 1894 they cost 50 cents each. The Edison phonograph cost $40 and was considered expensive, but the first coin-in-the-slot nickelodeon had been invented in 1892.

Portrait of a City: Berlin in the 1890s

A MODEST provincial town in the mid 19th century, Berlin by 1900 had become a great imperial city, with a population approaching 3 million inhabitants and a great avenue, Unter den Linden, which could stand comparison with Paris's Champs Elysées. Its richest and most successful citizens were moving into new apartment buildings on the Kurfurstendamm, or building large and expensive villas around the Grunewald forest and on the shores of the Wansee and the Havel. The new Reichstag on the Konigplatz, completed in 1894, was the largest of many magnificent public buildings erected to mark the city's imperial status.

Much of this new building was ostentatious, often mocked by Berliners themselves. When the new Siegesallee or Victory Way – a promenade lined by 32 marble statues of the Kaiser's ancestors carved by Rheinhold Begas – was completed in 1901, Berliners boasted that Begas was the worst sculptor in the world. A cartoon of the time shows visitors gazing at the statues and saying: 'My, how beautiful everything is here! Even the bird droppings are made of marble!'

The new Berlin had its admirers. Mark Twain, visiting in the 1890s, wrote: 'It is a new city ... Chicago would seem venerable beside it ... There is no other city in the country, whose streets are so generally wide ... Only parts of

IMPERIAL CITY   Kaiser Wilhelm is driven along Unter den Linden in the early 1900s while (left) statues of his ancestors tower over ordinary citizens on the Siegesallee.

Chicago are stately and beautiful, whereas all of Berlin is stately and substantial, and it is not merely in parts but uniformly beautiful.'

The world's first electric trams, built by Siemens, appeared in the 1880s, along with the first lines of the city's elevated railway. In 1902 Berlin opened its first underground railway line, two years ahead of New York City.

Berliners knew how to enjoy their city. They strolled in the Tiergarten, picnicked in the Grunewald, or joined the *Bummel*, the leisurely promenade along

Unter den Linden. They ate at Kempinski's, where half a dozen oysters or a glass of sparkling wine could be had for 75 pfennigs. If that was too expensive, they could eat at one of the Aschinger chain of Bierstuben, where a sandwich cost 10 pfennigs.

Berlin was also an industrial city, and Berliners boasted that it had the worst slums in the world. However, enlightened industrialists, such as Siemens, were building factories on greenfield sites and creating model suburbs around them for their employees. And Berlin's poorer citizens could enjoy the garden colonies around the outskirts, which they tended at weekends.

SCHOOLS OF ARCHITECTURE Glasgow Art School was designed by Charles Rennie Mackintosh, but the influence of William Morris, as in Wightwick Manor (right), begun in 1887, was probably longer-lasting in Britain.

a style that reflected the function of the building and the materials and construction methods used.

The Deutscher Werkbund, founded in Munich in 1907, was dedicated to a functional aestheticism in the design of household appliances, furniture and fabrics. Otto Wagner's *Moderne Architektur*, first published in 1896, was very influential, and its principles were realised in his own Vienna Postal Savings Building, completed in 1906. Frank Lloyd Wright's low-slung, functional 'prairie houses', which made no historical reference, but expressed instead their site, structure and materials, were greatly admired by European architects.

It was department stores and factories that were the first buildings to show the effects of the new

TRULY MODERN This interior of a house designed by Frank Lloyd Wright has the clean, functional lines that were characteristic of his exteriors.

UNDERGROUND STYLE The entrance to a Paris Metro station shows the influence of Art Nouveau in its design.

EXTREMISTS This exterior of a house designed by Antoni Gaudi defies stylistic classification. At the other extreme, the work (left) of his near-contemporary, the British potter William de Morgan, was more Pre-Raphaelite than modernist.

thinking. The Wertheim store in Berlin (1896) and the Tietz department store in Dusseldorf (1908) were among the first to show something like pure functionalism in their design. In France, A.G. Perret built the first all-concrete building in 1903. In Germany, Peter Behrens designed the first major functional factory – the AEG Turbine Building in Berlin. As early as 1911, Walter Gropius, who later founded the Bauhaus School, built the Fagus factory at Alfeld am Leine, which, with its steel frame, glass façade, flat roof and complete absence of ornamentation, was a forerunner of the International Modernist architecture of the 1920s and 1930s.

Although the idea of purely functional architecture and design was well established before the outbreak of war in 1914, it had not captured the public imagination, and only a few examples of it could actually be seen. Most new buildings in the early 1900s were still heavily ornamented in one historical style or another, and most manufactured articles – with such rare exceptions as the bicycle and the Ford motor car – were still automatically given a highly decorated appearance; even such highly functional articles as sewing machines and typewriters were covered in elaborate gilt scrolling.

LAMPLIGHT AT TIFFANY'S The Tiffany 'Dragonfly' table lamp epitomises the Art Nouveau style, still popular in 1914.

THE WORLD OF WORK

With its giant factories and cottage industries, its new technologies

and age-old crafts, its office workers, peasants and domestic servants, the world of

work was one of extreme contrasts.

COTTAGE INDUSTRY A group of straw plaiters in Bedfordshire, England, make hats from local straw.

NOTHING sums up the contrasts of the Western world at the dawn of the 20th century more vividly than people's working lives. On the one hand, as the department store and mail-order catalogues of the time show, the industrialised areas were producing an astonishing range and variety of consumer goods. On the other hand, there were communities in Europe, and some in North America too, that were still largely self-sufficient, growing their own food, making their own bread, cheese, wine and beer, and buying their clothes and footwear, their furniture, household utensils and tools, from local craftsmen in the local market.

There were vast factories, powered by electricity, using mass-production assembly-line techniques, and vast corporations with complex management structures; Ford at Detroit employed 14 000 workers, Krupp of Essen employed nearly 70 000. There were new industries such as petrochemicals, electrical equipment, telecommunications, motor-vehicle manufacture and early synthetic materials. Yet millions were still employed as peasant proprietors, or seasonally hired farm labourers, as domestic servants, or as artisans in tiny family craft businesses. Between these two extremes, most manual workers still worked in small, privately owned factories employing fewer than 40 'hands'; in France, 60 per cent of workers were employed in establishments with fewer than ten, and the typical factory of the time was more like a collection of craftsmen's shops than an integrated industrial plant. The older industries, such as textiles or pottery, although often grouped in one place, were still mainly based on scores of small businesses of this kind.

From the 1890s on, there was a new industrial revolution, based on the application of electrical power and chemistry to industry, along with the introduction of the internal combustion engine and the development of assembly-line production techniques. In addition, the precision that had once been found only in such trades as clock-making was now being applied to the production of complex items such as sewing machines and motor cars.

In the booming world economy of the early 1900s, electricity played the role that the steam engine and the railways had done earlier in the 19th century. Leaders in the manufacture of equipment for the generation and application of electrical power were the United States and Germany, where Emil Rathenau founded the giant company AEG (Allgemeine Elekrizitats Gesellschaft). Britain, formerly the 'work-shop of the world' and the leading exporter of manufactures, found herself displaced from that position.

In the United States, the amount of electricity used rose tenfold between 1899 and 1914. By 1910 every large city in Europe and North and South America had been supplied with electric power for lighting and public transport. And although electricity could be generated from water, 90 per cent of it was still derived from coal. The coal-miner was a key worker in the industrial economy; there were almost 2 million of them in Britain and Germany.

Mass-production techniques had been developed during the

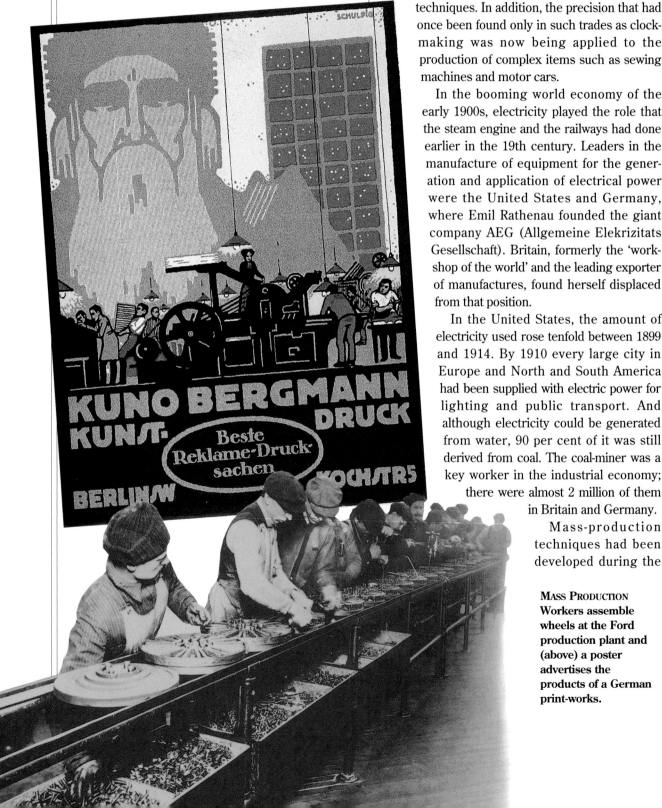

MASS PRODUCTION
Workers assemble wheels at the Ford production plant and (above) a poster advertises the products of a German print-works.

STEEL AND COAL Large factories such as the giant Krupp steelworks at Essen ran on the new power source, electricity. Right: British coal-miners emerge from their shift. The new manufacturing processes depended on coal for power.

American Civil War in response to the urgent and large-scale need for weapons, clothing and shoes. In craft manufacture, a handful of craftsmen and apprentices are responsible for making an entire article from start to finish. In mass production, the article – a rifle, for example – is broken down into its component parts; these parts are turned out in large numbers with the help of machine tools, and then assembled. Mass production, combined with new ideas about scientific management developed in the United States, changed the nature of work: the workman became an animate machine, part of the work process and compelled to keep pace with it, whereas the skilled craftsman had himself set the pace. But the results were startling, especially when combined with the moving assembly line, which brought the parts to the assembly worker. When this was installed at the Ford factory in Detroit, production of Model T cars rose to 1000 a day by 1914, and the time taken to produce a single car fell from 12 hours in 1913 to just over 90 minutes in 1914.

These new production methods called for heavy capital investment, and therefore required high output in order to be economical. Mass markets

HORSEPOWER

Each of London's horse-drawn omnibuses required the services of ten horses, each of which ate 21 lb (9.5 kg) of oats and hay a day. The manufacturers of the first 'horseless carriages' emphasised how cheap they were to run.

DAIRY MAIDS Women workers in a commercial dairy. Milk was produced by town herds for supplying urban populations.

A PROBLEM FOR THE POSTMAN

By the end of the 19th century, it seemed that there was no limit to what could be bought by mail order. In his catalogue, William Cooper of London offered 'hospitals dispatched within twenty-four hours of the receipt of order and erected complete for occupation within fourteen days'. The hospitals were made of a new product, corrugated iron.

had to be found so that goods could be sold in volume. This, in turn, required that a substantial percentage of the population had some disposable income after providing for basic needs such as food and accommodation. By the early 1900s, a typical British workman would be spending 40 per cent of his wages on food for himself and his family, and his equivalent in France or Germany would be spending over 50 per cent; the average American worker, on the other hand, needed only 25 per cent of his wages to feed his family. The

EYEWITNESS

TEMPTATIONS OF THE NEW DEPARTMENT STORES

IN AN ARTICLE in the *Fortnightly Review* of 1896, Lady Jeune wrote about the pleasures, and the dangers, of shopping in the great department stores of the time:

❛ We are not able to stand against the overwhelming temptations which besiege us at every turn ... We go to purchase something we want; but when we get to our shop there are so many fascinating things that we never thought of till they presented their obtrusive fascinations on every side. We look for a ribbon, a flower, a chiffon of some sort or other, and we find ourselves in a Paradise of ribbons, flowers, and chiffons, without which our life becomes impossible and our gown unwearable. There are many shops in London into which one cannot safely trust oneself. There are the drawbacks of noise, heat, and overcrowding, but they are more than counter-balanced by the brightness of the electric light and the brilliancy of the colours, and the endless variety on every side. There are two very important changes which contribute to the temptation of spending money nowadays. One is the gathering together under one roof of all kinds of goods – clothing, millinery, groceries, furniture, in fact all of the necessities of life ... What an amount of trouble and expense is avoided where one can order one's New Zealand mutton downstairs, buy one's carpet on the ground floor, and deck oneself out in all the glory of Worth or La Ferrier on the top floor, to all of which one is borne on the wings of a lift, swift and silent. ❜

COME AND BUY Advertisements became more colourful and sophisticated. Soap and, in Germany, electrical goods were subjects for major campaigns, while mail-order catalogues offered a huge range of items, from crockery to cars.

beginnings of a consumer society, therefore, were seen first in the United States, and to a lesser extent in Britain, Australia, New Zealand and Canada, with continental Europe lagging behind.

THE RETAILING REVOLUTION

One of the first signs of a consumer boom was a huge increase in the volume and scale of advertising, soap manufacturers such as Pears being among the first to use display advertising. Another development was the introduction of selling on credit, for example for sewing machines, furniture and electrical goods, as manufacturers realised that the market would not grow quickly enough if people had to save up beforehand for these relatively expensive goods. To stimulate consumption still further, door-to-door salesmen were now calling on housewives to demonstrate household appliances.

Another development, still peculiar to the Anglo-Saxon world before the First World War, was the growth of chain grocery stores, for example the Great Atlantic and Pacific Tea Company in the United States and the Lipton chain in Britain; Lipton had 245 shops by 1898 and its founder, Sir Thomas Lipton, was rich enough to become a leading yachtsman and host to King Edward VII

and George V. Other familiar British stores such as W.H. Smith, Boots, Sainsbury's and Marks and Spencer also started life at this time, as did Woolworth's, which had 1000 of its 'five and ten cent stores' in the United States by 1911. In Britain the Cooperative movement, which aimed to give working-class people the benefit of bulk purchasing and a 'dividend' from its profits, was founded in the North of England. In the United States, mail-order selling by catalogue served isolated rural communities; the huge illustrated

continued on page 38

SHOPKEEPERS Most French shops, such as this Parisian chemist, were privately owned.

PALACE OF CONSUMPTION

LONDON'S Harrods was typical of the great European and American department stores of the turn of the century. They were magnificently designed, and offered their customers almost every kind of goods from groceries to high fashion to household necessities and furniture. But as well as tempting the eye, they provided places for rest and refreshment, so that shoppers had no reason to leave the premises before their shopping day was done.

OFFICE LIFE British clerks (all male) work in serried ranks. Left: The new type of office building was purpose-built, and organised on industrial lines for maximum efficiency.

catalogues of Sears and Roebuck, which was the biggest of many mail-order companies, included an astonishing variety of goods, ranging from agricultural implements and furniture to clothing, footwear and appliances. Goods began to be packaged and branded, and American and British consumers became familiar with such brands as Quaker Oats, Kellogg, Campbells, Heinz, Swift and Armour. The poorer classes also grew accustomed to buying inexpensive factory-made shoes and clothing rather than resorting to craftsman shoemakers, tailors and seamstresses.

Department stores, which had been established since the 1860s on the model of Paris's Bon Marché of 1852, grew bigger and more splendid. In the great American cities, in particular, theatre designers were hired to decorate stores, and no expense was spared to make them magnificent. Interiors were furnished with coloured glass, fountains and brilliant lighting. Orchestras played continuously and fashion shows were presented to entertain customers.

IN THE OFFICE

As industries grew and became more complex, and as the state intervened in more and more areas of life, there was an enormous growth in the number of 'white collar' managerial and clerical jobs. The mid-Victorian clerk had enjoyed a certain status, working closely with his employer, trusted by him and respected for his skills. By the 1900s, however, the clerical worker was more likely to be working

A REVOLUTION IN KEEPING PAPERS.

The CERES Reminder

(Registered)

Stands on Desk or Table and keeps Papers in order and free from dust.

The blank Cards of the dividing Guides can be headed according to individual requirements, and the Tablet for a Month's Engagements is washable.

PRICE.

With 9 Guides with movable cards, 10s. 6d.; Extra Guides, 6d. each or 5s. per dozen; Postage and Packing, 1s.

The CERES system can be had in Boxes, Drawers, Cabinets, Standing Desks, Writing Tables, &c., on any scale, for private, professional and commercial use. See Illustrated Pamphlet, post free.

THE CERES DEPOT *for High-Class Time-Saving Appliances,*

PAPERWORK Office equipment manufacturers aimed to satisfy the craving for business efficiency.

with a roomful of others of similar status, managed by a supervisor and remote from his employer. The introduction of the typewriter in the 1880s brought women into the office for the first time, and by 1911 they constituted a quarter of all clerical workers in the advanced industrial countries.

In the United States, the principles of division of labour and scientific management that had been developed in factories were being applied in offices. Clerks were divided into departments, each of which carried out only one stage of a work process, with every clerk in a department doing the same work. Where the Victorian clerk had been the equivalent of a craftsman, responsible for the whole of a transaction, the clerk in an American office was a process worker – a change symbolised by the introduction of the time clock into offices in the 1900s.

American manuals on the scientific management of office routines promised remarkable increases in efficiency; if the task of opening the mail, for example, were given to a single

OFFICE TECHNOLOGY
Typewriting machines revolutionised office work. They were increasingly used by women workers, who were known as type-writers.

clerk trained in the most efficient time-and-motion method, the rate of letter-opening could be increased from 20 an hour to between 100 and 300 an hour.

Similar principles were applied to the design of office furniture, to make it comfortable and efficient, and at the same time to reduce the office-worker's privacy; the 19th-century roll-top desk, for example, gave way to the modern flat-topped table with side-drawers. Clerks were encouraged to keep their stationery and other working tools in standardised locations, so that they could be found at a moment's notice, and standardisation was applied even to the sort of pen-nibs to be used. Scientific management theories led in the 1910s to the use in American offices of dictating machines, based on the Edison phonograph, as a means of eliminating the combined role of the shorthand typist, which was believed to be inefficient.

ON THE LAND

In the years before the end of the 19th century, most people, even in industrialised countries, were still employed on the land, either as peasant smallholders or as labourers or rural craftsmen; only in Britain were more people employed in manufacturing than in agriculture before 1900. In Germany by the early 1900s, industry

39

FIELD WORK At the turn of the century, most agricultural work in Europe was still done by hand, as reflected in a painting of a group of French farmworkers bringing in the harvest. Left: German agricultural labourers pick potatoes.

had overtaken agriculture as the chief source of employment, but in most other European countries it still lagged behind. By 1914 only 8 per cent of the labour force in Britain worked on the land, compared with 35 per cent in Germany and 43 per cent in France.

Because Britain followed a policy of importing cheap food from abroad to feed her towns and cities (80 per cent of her wheat and over 40 per cent of her meat), British agriculture suffered a severe depression during these years, which was exacerbated between 1892 and 1895 by the worst drought in history. As locally produced wheat became an uneconomic crop from the 1890s onwards, Britain turned to stock and dairy farming, specialising also in market gardening, orchards, poultry rearing and potato production. The prominence in the British diet of fish and chips, brussels sprouts and cabbage, jams and jellies dates from this period.

As Britain's agricultural communities suffered, more and more townspeople were commuting from houses in the country or weekending there.

Here they lived cheek by jowl with cottagers, who were barely scraping a living from what was left of the common land, and whose way of life had scarcely changed since the 18th century. Farmworkers – men, women and children – still went to hiring fairs to wait to be taken on for a season's work, carrying the implements that were the badges of their various skills: as ploughmen, hedgers, horsemen, pigmen and so forth. Subtly, the social character of the British countryside was changing. Falling land values and rents forced many of the old landed gentry, who had traditionally been involved in local government, the magistracy and charitable works, either to sell up or to move what remained

HARD LABOUR The English farmworker was skilled but low paid.

THE LIFE OF A GERMAN FARM LABOURER

GERMANY IN the years around 1900 was, like France, mainly a land of small peasant proprietors, but in Prussia, east of the Elbe, there were great noble estates owned by Junker families and run on almost feudal lines.

Franz Rehbein, a labourer on one of these estates, later wrote his memoirs. He was one of six children left destitute when their father, a poor tailor, died of tuberculosis. At the age of 13, he was working with his mother in the potato harvest; he then took service as a 'farm boy'. For more than 20 years thereafter, he worked as a farm labourer, one of more than a million such workers in Germany at that time.

His recollections of his employers are favourable, on the whole, although he recalled one manager's wife who made a point of praising the hired men of the previous year, 'who always ate a very light breakfast'. His diet was monotonous: buckwheat groats, skimmed milk, fat bacon, black bread and potatoes. As a hired man, he was subject to the Prussian Servant's Code, which reduced farm workers to something approaching serfdom.

He was forbidden to leave the estate in the evening to visit a neighbouring village without the overseer's permission. If he decided to leave his employment before the expiry of his contract, he could be arrested and forcibly returned to the estate. On one occasion, he lost an entire year's wages when an employer charged him with negligence resulting in the loss of a farm animal. There was, of course, no sickness or accident insurance or any retirement benefit.

At the age of 30, after three years' service in the cavalry, Rehbein married a farm girl – but only, as was the custom of the time, when it became necessary to legalise their relationship because she was pregnant with their first child. He now became a 'free'

COUNTRY FOLK
For German farm workers in 1900 much of the work was seasonal.

day labourer, which meant that he needed to earn enough in daily wages through the spring, summer and autumn to keep his family fed through the winter, when there was no employment. His annual income was probably never more than £80.

Rehbein's career was summarily brought to an end when his right arm was mangled in a steam-driven threshing machine and had to be amputated. With no compensation, and with his wife expecting a fourth child, he was saved from utter destitution when he became a minor official in the Social Democratic Party.

of their wealth into financial investments; to an extent they were replaced by wealthy newcomers, who lived in the community but had little connection with its everyday life.

In Europe, on the other hand, food production was protected by tariffs, and peasant agriculture prospered, especially after 1900 when world food prices turned sharply upwards. Peasant smallholders formed themselves into cooperatives for marketing their produce, obtaining credit and buying seed, implements and breeding stock. Improved roads and cheap transport helped them to get their produce to the market.

Agricultural colleges and experimental farms helped to make agriculture more scientific, especially in Germany, Scandinavia, Holland and Belgium. Sophisticated crop-rotation methods were used, along with fertilisers and improved farm implements such as milking machines, mowers, reapers, binders and steam threshers. France, meanwhile, remained relatively conservative, a country of small peasant proprietors, with

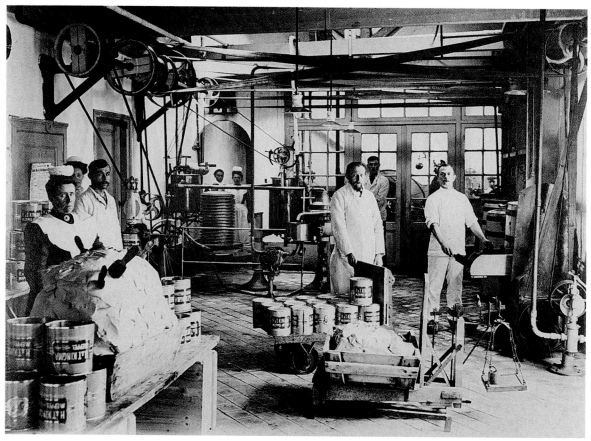

MODERN METHODS A mechanised Dutch dairy in 1911 places great importance on hygienic conditions.

more than 2 million holdings of 2½ acres (1 ha) or less. Yet the different soils and climates within its borders produced a huge variety of crops, including its world-famous cheeses and wines; and there was a profound stability about French country life that gave Frenchmen little incentive to emigrate, compared with the natives of other European countries.

The great wheat farms of North America led the world in mechanisation. A combine harvester hauled by mules was used in California in the late 1880s, and steam traction engines were commonly used as power units for many operations, such as threshing. The first successful petrol-driven tractor was built in 1892. By 1907 there were 600 of them in use in the United States;

thereafter, they began steadily to replace steam power and the horse. To fence off the farms of the Great Plains from the cattle ranches, American farmers used a recent invention – barbed wire. Meanwhile, the meat and dairy products of Australia, New Zealand and Argentina could now be transported thousands of miles in refrigerated ships, providing cheap food for the industrial populations of Britain and Europe.

DIGGING POWER Farm machinery was powered by steam, like this Darby Digger.

HOUSES AND HOMES

In the decades before the First World War, home could be a palatial

mansion, a comfortable house, a modern, purpose-built apartment, a damp,

unhealthy cottage or an overcrowded, disease-ridden slum.

TEA TIME Edwardian ladies take afternoon tea amid luxurious surroundings. In London's East End (inset) the food on the table is the only food in the house.

THERE NEVER had been, and never would be again, such a huge contrast between the homes of the very rich and those of the very poor as there was in the years before the First World War. At one extreme were the great town and country houses that the aristocracy could still afford to maintain and the vast palaces built by the New Rich, particularly in the United States; at the other, the disease-ridden slums in which the urban poor lived two or three to a room, the cellars in which many families were still raised, and the sometimes picturesque but generally insanitary hovels of the poorest peasants or farmworkers.

Between these two extremes, however, there was one feature of life common to the houses both of prosperous workers and wealthy middle-class people; and that was the tendency to idealise the home, to regard it as a sanctuary in which the family could shut itself off from the cares and cruelties of the outside world. As the workplace,

TASTE Part of the interior of Wightwick Manor (left). The wallpaper and furniture are inspired by William Morris. The design by Alphonse Mucha (right) was high fashion in 1902.

whether factory or office, became more functional, so the home became by contrast more and more a place to be decorated, ornamented and cherished.

The Victorian dislike of empty space and plain surfaces continued to dominate taste, and as factory-made ceramics, ornaments and furnishings proliferated, so the typical home became even more cluttered. As wage levels improved, working people used much of their surplus spending power to mimic the middle classes and fill their rooms with knick-knacks, wax flowers, patterned carpets, and tasselled and embroidered covers for every surface.

There were two influences that ran counter to the prevailing taste for ornamentation and clutter. One of these was the principle of 'art furnishing' or 'moral furnishing', which derived in part from the teaching and practice of William Morris. It called for a reduction in the amount of furniture so as to create more space in rooms. Heavily upholstered furniture was to give way to wooden-framed chairs and settees with loose cushions. The amount of decoration was to be reduced, and light colours chosen in place of dark or garish ones. Rugs on wooden floors were preferred to fitted carpets. Furniture, it was argued, should frankly reflect the materials from which it was made and the

HOME COMFORTS A typical middle-class sitting room of the 1890s. The Victorian impulse to decorate and cover surfaces was still strong.

HIDE THE PIANO

The piano was regarded by many people as an ugly piece of furniture, which should be concealed by drapes as far as possible. The writer on household matters, Mrs Panton, made for hers 'a very pretty frame of sage-green silk worked with rosebuds'.

KITCHENS OLD . . . **With its ornaments and comfortable chair, this French farmhouse kitchen also serves as a living room.**

craftsmanship of its manufacture. The British architect and designer Charles Voysey wrote in 1895 with disgust about 'the motley collection of forms and colours with which most rooms are crowded' and urged his readers to 'try the effect of a well-proportioned room, with whitewashed walls, plain carpet and simple oak furniture, and nothing in it but necessary articles of use, and one pure ornament in the form of a simple vase of flowers'. Rooms furnished in accordance with these principles at the end of the 19th century have a surprisingly modern, even a timeless appearance, but they were far from typical of their time.

Much more of its time was the fashion for Art Nouveau. For a brief period, between 1890 and 1910, and especially in continental Europe, this style produced some exquisite interiors, quite unlike anything seen before or since, in which every surface and every detail was designed as part of an aesthetic whole. But such interiors were the property of a wealthy few, employing men and women from the new profession of interior designer, and again far from representative of the way most people lived.

THE LIVING ROOM

For working-class people and for peasants, the centre of family life was the kitchen. This contained the hearth at which the cooking was done, a sink for washing if running water was available, and the table

. . . AND NEW **An electric oven of 1912. Very few homes would have possessed one.**

at which the family ate. There was often also a bed alcove in which some of them slept. If the household possessed a portable bath, it was brought into the kitchen and filled with hot water from the kitchen range.

Working-class people who could afford it had a sitting room or parlour, reserved for Sundays or for special visitors, such as the clergyman or the doctor, who were considered too grand to be admitted to the kitchen. By the end of the 19th century, this room would often contain a piano; in 1890 more than twice as many were being produced in England as in 1850, and they were being shipped in their thousands to countries such as Australia and New Zealand.

For middle-class people, the kitchen was the domain of the servants. In most homes, this was dominated by the kitchen range or 'kitchener', made of cast iron that had to be kept bright with blacking, and fitted with dampers for controlling and directing the heat. Kitcheners heated water for the household and generally held two ovens – one relatively cool, the other hot for roasting and baking. Gas cookers were available, and *Cassell's Book of the Household* (1897) recommended them for their convenience: 'They save an enormous

EYEWITNESS

A COUNTRY CHILDHOOD IN EDWARDIAN ENGLAND

LEONARD THOMPSON was one of the seven children of a farm labourer in the early 1900s:

❝ There were seven children at home and father's wages had been reduced to 10s a week. Our cottage was nearly empty – except for people. There was a scrubbed brick floor and just one rug made of scraps of old clothes pegged into a sack. The cottage had a living room, a larder and two bedrooms. Six of the boys and girls slept in one bedroom and our parents and the baby slept in the other. There was no newspaper and nothing to read except the Bible. All the village houses were like this.

Our food was apples, potatoes, swedes and bread, and we drank our tea without milk or sugar. Skim milk could be bought from the farm but it was thought a luxury. Nobody could get enough to eat no matter how they tried. Two of my brothers were out to work. One was eight years old and he got 3s a week, the other got about 7s. Our biggest trouble was water. There was no water near, it all had to be fetched from the foot of a hill nearly a mile away. "Drink all you can at school", we were told – there was a tap at school. You would see the boys and girls filling themselves up like camels before they left school so that they would have enough water to last the day. ❞

amount of time and trouble especially early in the morning. A servant can slip on a dress, or the master of the house his dressing gown, when, perhaps, the proper person has overslept herself, turn a tap, light a match and go back to his room, and by the time he has finished dressing, there is a large kettleful of boiling water ready for the use of the house.'

Gas fires were also available, but again the vast majority of rooms were heated by a coal or wood-burning stove or by an open fireplace, and it was still one of the early morning tasks of the lower servants to carry coal scuttles upstairs and to lay and light fires. By the end of the 19th century, fireplaces were fitted with hoods or canopies and with air regulators that allowed some control of temperature. The fashion was for tiled hearths and wooden fireplaces, often with mirrored over-mantels; the mantel itself was often covered in a tasselled and embroidered mantel-valance and loaded with ornaments. If the home was seen as a temple of domesticity, the drawing-room fireplace was its principal shrine.

Gaslight, which had replaced oil lamps and candles earlier in the 19th century, was just beginning to be replaced by electricity in wealthier houses. In this respect Britain, with its abundance of coal and therefore of coal-gas, lagged behind North America and Germany; but even so, in London alone there were an estimated 2.5 million electric lamps in use by the end of the century.

RINGING FOR THE SERVANTS

Modest homes might have their parlour; the houses of the well-to-do by contrast had many specialised rooms: not only a drawing room and dining room, but also a breakfast room, a library, perhaps a music room, a billiard room and a smoking room. (With the advent of the cigarette, smoking had become desegregated and smoking in the dining room was now permitted in many

DAILY ORDERS The mistress of a
French house instructs her cook.

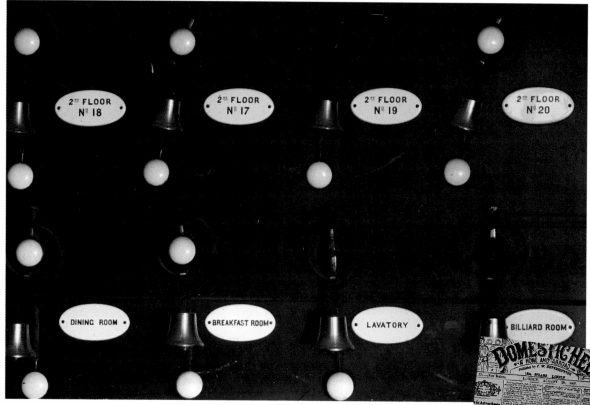

SUMMONED BY BELLS The householder could summon a servant, by means of bells, from any room in the house. Servants sought work through advertisements (right) or domestic service agencies.

houses, but it was still thought desirable to have a separate room in which men could smoke their pipes and cigars.) All of these rooms, and all the bedrooms, were linked with the servants' quarters by means of bell pulls, or in some cases by means of internal telephones or speaking tubes, for any substantial house in the years before the First World War was totally dependent on servants.

Domestic service was still one of the chief sources of employment. In England alone in 1901, there were 1.25 million indoor domestic servants, and one in every three girls between the ages of 15 and 20 was a

GRATE WORK Black-leading the grate was a daily task for the lower servants.

domestic servant. Only in the northern states of the United States, where industrialisation offered more alternatives to a form of employment regarded as menial, were overall numbers of domestic servants beginning to fall, and rich Americans employed quite as many servants as their European counterparts.

Lower middle-class people might employ a single maid-of-all-work, who might well suffer from the pangs of loneliness in addition to long hours, dreary work and wretched wages, but in the homes of the rich there were large numbers of servants with different ranks and skills. The very biggest households might employ 40 or 50 servants, ranging from the steward at the top of the hierarchy to the page or footboy and the scullery maid at the bottom. Male servants included the

DHOBI WALLAH An Indian laundry-servant stands with iron at the ready.

valet, the butler, the chef, the gardener and under-gardeners, the footmen (chosen for their height and good looks, and splendidly liveried), the coachman and grooms, the chauffeur and the stable boy, with wages ranging from £80 to £6 per annum. Female servants included the housekeeper, earning perhaps £40 per annum and often the most formidable figure in the household, the lady's maid, the cook, the nurse, upper and lower housemaids, the nurserymaid, the laundrymaid, the kitchenmaid, and the scullerymaid with wages of about £5 per annum. Each was expected to acquire his or her special skills, whether it was blacking the grate, carrying water for baths, polishing silver or caring for the master's or mistress's clothes. They were governed by a strict hierarchy. The most senior servants, such as the steward and housekeeper, had their own sitting rooms, but the others ate together in the servants' hall, sitting at table in accordance with their rank.

A middle or upper servant in a large household could enjoy the benefits of regular meals, modestly comfortable accommodation and the company of the other servants, plus perhaps the constant interest of observing the grand life 'upstairs'. A good master or mistress would value his or her servants and treat them with consideration and even with courtesy – 'It's only in second-class

EYEWITNESS

EDWARDIAN COMFORT

THE BRITISH writer Naomi Jacob recalls a typical day in an affluent Edwardian household:

❛ They began the day with a "hearty breakfast", which meant a full meal. Porridge, eggs and bacon or kidneys and bacon, great platefuls of home-fed ham and eggs "topped off" with buttered toast and homemade marmalade, and many huge cups of tea... My grandfather always ate a breakfast which consisted of chops or steaks, followed by eggs and ham, and drank a tankard – his own special silver tankard – or more of ale. They breakfasted early, half past seven or eight being regarded as a normal time... They lunched at half past one, alone with their wives and the elder children... A heavy meal liable to necessitate a short sleep afterwards. A modest household had soup and a joint, because the 'made up' dishes were regarded as unsuitable by the master of the house ... A sweet of some sort followed, and later cheese – Stilton, Cheshire, Wensleydale or Cheddar. At the end of the meal the mistress of the house might say tentatively, "Would you like a cup of tea?" Her spouse, having consumed light ale throughout the meal, usually made a sound like "Tea! Paff! Poo!" and retired ... Tea was a woman's meal, though the husband often "just dropped in" to the drawing room to do no more than drink a cup of tea, eat several slices of exquisitely thin bread and butter, a few small hot cakes and a piece of homemade plum, seed, sand, cherry or other variety of cake ... Dinner was preceded by glasses of sherry, in our household usually served in my father's study ... Dinner, which was served at some houses as early as seven but in more "advanced" homes at eight, was a meal of some formality. There was a rather stiffly laundered cloth – "double damask" ... and huge table-napkins calculated to slip off the most careful knees. [There was] Soup, fish and a joint which the husband carved ... There was always a "sweet", always cheese, and fruit "in season". ❜

MODERN HYGIENE
The American bathroom of 1909, complete with running water and a shower, represents the new obsession with hygiene. The paper-holder of 1894, on the other hand, represents the old obsession with decoration.

some masters, for example, insisted that lower servants turn their faces to the wall when they encountered members of the family or guests in the corridors of the house; most discouraged their servants from forming any attachments outside the house, even when the long working hours permitted them. And all servants were dependent on receiving good 'references' from their present employers, without which they had no hope of obtaining decent employment elsewhere.

THE BATHROOM
One of the social benchmarks of the period before the First World War was the possession – or not – of a bathroom. Working-class homes did not have bathrooms; in many cases they did not have a

houses,' said a London servant in 1889, 'that they treat servants without consideration. But it isn't everyone can get into a big house.' Even in the best of households there was no question that masters and servants were like distinct human species;

EYEWITNESS

THE ARRIVAL OF THE WC

The playwright Walter Greenwood was brought up in the North of England before the First World War. The family lived near the poverty line. He recalls the lavatories of the time:

❛ Springtime and, with the warmer days, another stench added to the already tainted air, the expanding effluvium of countless privies in this place where main drainage was unknown. . . .

Spring, the time for the annual clean-up assault by fathers and dutiful grown-up sons. The prescription was time-honoured and invariable: three-pennyworth of thirsty quicklime put into the tin bath, buckets of water thrown on it so that it boiled, bounced and rattled, then, when it had settled, a bag of blue thrown in. All hands on deck with brushes in stinking "petties" and fetid middens and on faded backyard walls, both inside and out, until all were dazzlingly transformed by thick coats of sweet-smelling whitewash.

Now, in the quiet of night when the moon was at the full, a fragile and heart-lifting beauty haunted the back entries. The custom persisted even after modern hygiene banished the tin privies, replacing these with what was called "the WC", a thing of wonderment to juvenile minds. Marvellous! A box full of water which refilled itself no matter how many times the chain was pulled, nor did it ever spill over. The novelty quickly palled. ❜

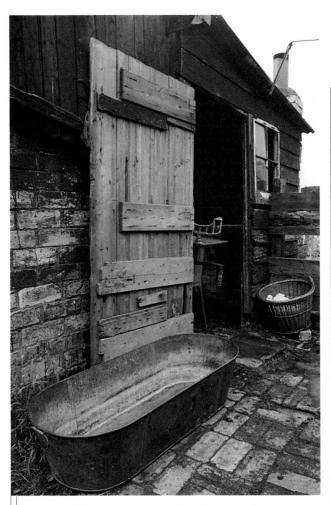

PUBLIC BATHS A communal bath and wash house in an English mining village.

bath of any kind, but would use the local public baths. Most middle-class houses and apartments by the 1900s did have purpose-built bathrooms. Some very grand houses, however, were built in those years without any bathrooms – for the simple reason that the bedroom or dressing room was still considered to be the proper place for a bath to be fitted.

The Victorians ornamented and decorated their baths and their bathrooms as they did everything

A TUB OF TOOTHPASTE

For most of the 19th century, toothpaste was available only in pots, usually made of glazed earthenware. The first flexible metal toothpaste tube was devised by a dentist, Dr Washington Sheffield, of New London, Connecticut, in 1892. In Britain, Beecham's Tooth Paste was retailed in tubes from the same year.

else in their homes. But, in the early 1900s, a new obsession with hygiene led to the practice of stripping away the panelling from around the bath and exposing its legs, with the result that the bathroom began to take on something like its modern functional appearance. At the same time, with improvements in sewerage systems, the flush water closet had become well established, and WCs, which had hitherto been banished to basements or backyards, were being installed in bathrooms. This practice was condemned by *Cassell's Book of the Household*, which referred to 'the objectionable practice of placing a WC in the bathroom . . . common to suburban houses'. Working-class people rarely, if ever, had indoor lavatories; instead, they were expected to share outside privies.

Even in great houses, although taps were becoming more common, water for washing often had to be carried in buckets by servants. Bedrooms were provided with marble-topped washstands, on which were placed a basin and soap dish and jugs for hot and cold water, while a towel-horse stood nearby.

COSTUME AND FASHION

The period known to the French as the *belle époque* was one of great elegance, at least as far as the upper classes were concerned. Typical of women's fashion was the 'Gibson Girl', created by the artist Charles Dana Gibson; the Gibson Girl's S-bend figure was produced by the corsetry of the time, which thrust the bosom forward while throwing back the hips. The bustle, still fashionable in the 1880s, disappeared in the last decade of the century. Skirts in the 1890s were long and often fitted with a train, even during the day. Day dresses were high at the neck, often with a boned collar, but evening dresses were generously décolleté. A

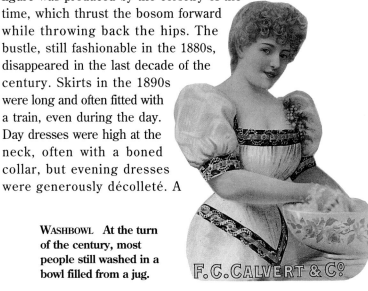

WASHBOWL At the turn of the century, most people still washed in a bowl filled from a jug.

F.C.CALVERT & C?

HEIGHT OF FASHION The house of Worth was one of the leading Paris fashion houses in the 1890s. **Left:** Corsetry produced the 'hour-glass' figure, as shown in 1906 by the actress Camille Clifford. **Far left:** Within a few years, some women had abandoned the corset in favour of a more comfortable and practical look.

street, was considered highly erotic. Lingerie, which had been severely practical in Victorian times, became glamorous, made in delicate colours and covered in lace and ribbons, perhaps reflecting the looser morals of the time. The hair was worn long and piled high on the head; and hats, still quite small in the 1890s, became steadily larger in the 1900s, when there was a rage for feathers, particularly egret feathers and ostrich plumes.

Fashion designers, and in particular French fashion designers, flourished during the *belle époque*. One of them, Paul Poiret, helped bring about a sharp change in women's fashions in the years immediately before the outbreak of war.

fashionable evening gown could be hugely expensive, representing hours of labour by the seamstress and the embroiderer. Much lace was worn, particularly on evening dresses and on petticoats, the display of which, when the woman lifted her long skirt to cross the

MASCULINE FRESHNESS The gentleman's cloakroom at Wightwick Manor has fitted basins and a general air of spaciousness and comfort. Right: Men were increasingly using toiletries such as talcum powder.

Colours became more striking; patterns took on an oriental flavour; rigid bodices gave way to softer drapery; lace fastenings gave way to buttons; and skirts became narrow at the hem. In their extreme form, such skirts became the 'hobble skirt', which severely restricted the wearer's step – to 3 in (7.5 cm) at most.

Running counter to the elaborate and showy fashions of the time, however, there was also a taste, particularly among younger middle-class women, for tailored coats-and-skirts, often made by men's tailors. The progressive young 'New Woman' of the time favoured a simple, almost mannish outfit, consisting of a plain straw hat, a high-necked, shirt-waist blouse and a long, plain skirt cinched with an elasticated belt.

For gentlemen, it was still incorrect to wear anything other than a frock coat or morning coat when making formal visits in town, but on other occasions the lounge suit was becoming more acceptable. An observer at London's Charing Cross Station in 1897 noted 'nearly two lounge suits to one morning coat and quite three lounges to one frock coat'. Trousers were worn narrow, and

young men were starting to wear them with creases in front – maintained by a new invention, the trouser press – and with permanent turnups.

Collars grew higher and higher in the 1890s and early 1900s, and cravats steadily gave way to neckties or bow ties. Beards went out of fashion for younger men, although moustaches were popular. Most men shaved, or were shaved, with an open 'cut-throat' razor, but the first Gillette safety razor blade appeared in 1904. Shampoo, introduced first in France, became increasingly fashionable in the 1890s.

In the evening, the tailcoat was still *de rigueur* on formal occasions, but increasingly men wore dinner jackets when dining at home or at their clubs. In the country, they might wear

MALE ELEGANCE French evening dress of the early 1900s was formal and elegant.

DEBUT OF THE TUXEDO

The Tuxedo takes its name from the Tuxedo Park Country Club, New York, where Griswold Lorillard first wore a short black coat with satin revers, modelled on the English smoking jacket, at the Autumn Ball on October 10, 1886. Until the First World War the dinner jacket, although increasingly popular, was regarded as suitable only for informal, men-only occasions. Introduced in Britain in 1888, it was known there at first as the 'dress lounge'. The term 'dinner jacket' did not become usual until the late 1890s.

HATS AND HAIR

The writer on fashion James Laver wrote that: 'Hats and hair . . . are very much more susceptible to influences of the day even than dress.' No man, however poor, would dream of going out of doors without covering his head, and hats and caps came in a wide variety of styles: top hats, bowlers, Homburgs, trilbys, straw hats, tweed hats and caps. Each type of headgear could convey a message about social class or about the occasion on which it was worn. Top hats were essential for formal dress, but were also worn by public officials. The Homburg, named after the spa town, became particularly successful in the 1890s after the Prince of Wales was seen wearing one. The bowler, named after the London hatter, William Bowler, steadily replaced the top hat among gentlemen in the City, but was also part of the 'Sunday best' dress of British working men. The flat cap

CLOSE SHAVES It was still usual for a man to be shaved by a barber, but from 1904 on he could shave himself with a Gillette safety razor (right).

was regarded as the badge of the working class.

Much attention was paid to men's hair, which was generally short and often dressed in scented oil. The use of shampoo became fashionable in the

HATS ON A variety of hats are worn by employees of the Great Western Railway on a trip to the Wye Valley.

1890s, with France leading the way.

Older men still wore Victorian beards and side-whiskers, but young men in the 1890s and 1900s preferred the moustache, clipped neatly in military fashion. Only a minority of men went completely clean-shaven. Gentlemen shaved daily, but for many men a weekly visit to the barber's shop was thought sufficient. The invention of the safety razor, however, probably encouraged more frequent shaving.

Norfolk jackets or light flannel or linen suits.

Official reports for Britain suggested that by 1904 working men were spending as much as 12 per cent of their income on clothes; and ready-made clothing became steadily more available during the period, particularly in the United States, where it could be bought from mail order catalogues. Nevertheless, it was still the case that a working-class man might well have one suit of clothes made for him in early manhood, and wear it on special occasions for the rest of his life, wearing castoffs for work.

FAMILY LIFE

During the early years of the 20th century, as society in Europe and North America became increasingly urbanised and industrialised, people worried about the decline of family life; family values, however, remained strong. The home was regarded with almost religious veneration, and the view that it was the proper place for a woman still prevailed among the majority of people. Nevertheless, relations between husband and wife, and parents and children, were becoming more relaxed and informal.

THE FAMILY IN 1900

Although families were becoming smaller, family ties remained strong, and the importance of the home as the focus of family life and activities increased. In addition, there was a growing tendency to regard marriage as being more to do with love and friendship than financial support.

IN THE EARLY 20th century, people worried about the decline of family life and 'family values' in an era of rapid urbanisation and industrialisation. And just as now, there were even calls for legislation to preserve the family unit as the foundation of a healthy society.

In general, in urban societies families were getting smaller, with, typically, three or four children rather than the five or more of mid-Victorian times. More and more people were marrying later or even going through life without ever marrying; the bachelor life represented in fiction by Sherlock Holmes, with his housekeeper and comfortable masculine quarters, was not at all uncommon and would not have attracted comment. More people were living alone, whether as young men and women who had left home to go to work or as elderly widows or widowers.

The extended family, with three generations living in the same house, might still be found in traditional rural societies, but had become rare in towns and cities. Even affluent working people were sometimes reluctant to take in elderly relatives, perhaps because at a time of rapid cultural change they were uncomfortable living with a grandparent who retained the coarser speech, manners and sanitary habits of an

OLD-AGE PENSIONS

An old-age pension scheme was introduced in Germany by Bismarck in 1889 and came into effect in 1891. The pension was payable to persons over 70 years of age who had contributed for at least 30 years.

The first country in the British Commonwealth to introduce a pension scheme was New Zealand, where pensions became payable in 1899. The New Zealand scheme was noncontributory; male applicants had to be 65, females 60, of good character, and with at least 25 years' residency in the country.

A British pension scheme was introduced by Lloyd George in his 1908 Budget and came into effect on January 1, 1909 amid scenes of nationwide rejoicing. One old woman in Walworth, London, offered the postmaster two rashers of bacon as thanks for his help in filling out the necessary forms.

A pension scheme was not introduced in the US until the 1930s.

earlier age. As a result, a very large number of elderly people, particularly elderly single men, were living in institutions such as the workhouse right up to the First World War. On the other hand, it was very usual for grandparents, brothers, sisters and other kinfolk to live very near each other in the same street, and very common for young children to be looked after by an aunt or grandmother while their mother went out to work. Where families were very large, children were quite often fostered or virtually adopted by a childless aunt or uncle.

So, although the nuclear family of parents and children had become the norm in towns and cities, it tended to merge into a larger family network, which itself merged with a neighbourhood community. Country people who moved into the cities or emigrated to the New World in the 1890s and 1900s tended to take with them their community structures and their own customs, rituals, religious festivals and family traditions. In addition, they probably had newspapers and theatre in their own language. People from the same area in Italy, for example, would share the same neighbourhood in New York, and the street replaced the village market as the place for gossip and

HARDSHIP A family in London's East End in 1912 struggles to make ends meet. The father clutches a handful of pawn tickets.

social encounters. Family ties remained strong. The sense of the alienated individual, isolated from the rest of society, that was to become a common theme later in the 20th century, was probably not something experienced by many people in the early 1900s.

In the years before the First World War, even families of quite modest means employed servants, and in some countries, long-term servants came to be regarded as almost a part of the family. Even in Britain, where master-servant relations were normally very formal, servants were expected to join the family at morning prayers, and an elderly nanny could be thought of by the family as almost

HAPPY FAMILY A New York family, on holiday at a lakeside resort, represent the smaller family unit that was becoming common in urban societies.

HOMELESS This New Yorker, homeless and jobless, lives in a damp cellar with several others.

contracts. The family still played its part, too, in determining occupations, which very often passed from father to son, whether as clergyman, army officer, coalminer or craft worker.

For the landed gentry and aristocracy, the family was still an important mechanism for the conservation of property, and the very rich saw marriage as a means of combining, and thus increasing, property or of tying new wealth to old titles. The 'season' in high society was very much a marriage market in which husbands, suitable in either birth or wealth, could be found for young women who were 'coming out'. Fortunes were spent by parents on giving grand balls and on ensuring that their daughters could be present, suitably and splendidly attired, at all the appropriate occasions during the Season. In the great cities, a whole economy made up of thousands of craft workers – dressmakers, hat makers, glove makers, jewellers – was based on dressing the upper classes for the pleasures of the Season.

one of them. Children, too, often formed close attachments, not only with their nannies and nursemaids, but with the other household servants as well.

THE ECONOMICS OF MARRIAGE

For farmers and for the millions of people who still worked from their homes as shopkeepers or craftsmen, the family was still a productive unit. Male and female roles differed: on the farm, while her husband tended the livestock and raised crops, the wife might look after the chickens and the vegetable garden, as well as taking care of the children and attending to the cooking; in a shop, she might help her husband serve at the counter and do the bookkeeping. But both men and women played their parts in the enterprise.

In Britain and in parts of Europe, whole families hired themselves out as farm labourers on annual

However, the marriages that were made as a result were nearly always based on a careful calculation of the pedigree, wealth and landed property of the parties involved. In that respect, the aristocracy was not so very different from the European peasantry, whose view of marriage was often equally unsentimental.

In contrast, middle-class British and American people surprised Europeans with their apparent indifference to the financial aspects of a marriage contract. The French writer Hippolyte Taine noted that the British middle class in general seemed

BACHELORS Young unmarried men often shared lodgings.

URTSHIP An English farm
ourer woos his
eetheart on the way to
rk.

to be indifferent to the long-term conservation of wealth and that, in contrast with their French counterparts, they seemed to seek money in order to spend it – on houses, holidays, expensive education for their children, servants, carriages, fashionable clothing and ample food and drink.

Although thrift and frugality were still strongly upheld as major principles of life, middle-class British and American families at this time had already entered an era of conspicuous consumption. In the United States the consumer ethic was spreading even to the working classes, a process made possible by higher wages and stimulated by mass advertising.

HOME SWEET HOME

As people got richer, the home was increasingly seen as a centre of leisure and family companionship and as a place for the display of material acquisitions – a novelty for the more prosperous working class. This new kind of leisured family lifestyle was especially evident in the suburbs that were springing up around the cities, particularly in the United States.

Cosmopolitan magazine in 1903 claimed that the suburb offered a 'compromise for those who temper an inherent or cultivated taste for green fields . . . with an unwillingness to entirely forego the delights of urban gaiety'. The whole idea of

'urban gaiety' as something for respectable people to enjoy was a new one. But at the same time, the new suburbanites were anxious to protect their exclusive communities from the unsavoury elements of the inner city. The *Cosmopolitan* article went on: 'The householder can rely upon quite a rigid enforcement of the restrictions designed to ensure the erection in the suburbs of residences of

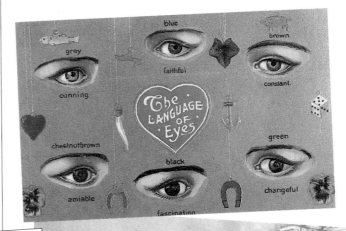

ROMANCE This German couple seem to take a solemn view of marriage, whereas the popular media (top right) encouraged more romantic ideas. The bicycle (above), which had recently been invented, allowed young people to meet unchaperoned.

THE PROBLEMS OF SETTING UP HOME

HOMEMAKING In the *Girls' Own Paper* young women pursue traditional household tasks.

M.V. Hughes, an English schoolteacher who became a trainer of teachers, was a typical 'New Woman' of the 1890s. In 1897 she married a young lawyer and her views on the roles of husband and wife seem to have been traditional:

❝ Most newly married women have the same difficulties to meet: servants or the lack of them; finding good provision shops; keeping expenditure down; making the daily routine run smoothly in the new surroundings. I had my share of these, and made a fair crop of mistakes.

We returned from Salisbury on the Monday afternoon, and spent the rest of the day in pottering about the flat, putting up pictures, sitting on packing cases, and revelling in the bare fact of having a home of our own. For supper we went out to a little restaurant. Miss Roger's present had been a large lamp, and fortunately I had laid in a supply of oil; it was therefore possible for Arthur to sit up and have a last go at his brief for the next day. So it was not till the following morning that my troubles began.

There was no gas in the flat (nor ever was for the seven years we lived in it). Now I had been accustomed to do marvels on the little gas ring in the Ladies' Chambers – cook porridge, fry bacon, scramble eggs, and even make a stew. And here I was faced with a huge iron range for my first attempt at a breakfast. Disraeli said there were three things a man should never grumble at because they were unalterable – the weather, his wife, and the kitchen range. But I think he would have let loose a few expressions if he had been in my shoes. I had got up early, lit the fire, filled the kettle, arrayed slices of bacon in the pan, only to be met by smoke billowing forth at me from my "fire". In despair I called out to Arthur for help. He just shoved a damper or two about, and that impish range, seeing a man on the job, gave up its tricks and blazed up brightly ...

everything began to hum – kettle began to sing, bacon began to frizzle, cloth was laid, and, best of all, Arthur had been got out of bed in good time.

As soon as he had started for the Temple I was busy enough. Most of my time was spent in unpacking cases, pushing things into place, and tidying away the oceans of packing paper and straw that surged around ... Then there was the servant's room to get ready, for she was to come on the following day. I had a rooted idea that a servant's bedroom must have pink chintz covered with muslin round her table. With some trouble I managed to buy these things beforehand; and now I had but to nail them onto a little table, make up her trestle bed, and lay out her caps and aprons. ...

Emma was a treasure. She not only knew how to work, but knew what to work at – a still more valuable asset. For I was ignorant in this line. I had vague ideas that servants were busy all the time, but what they were busy at was a mystery. Emma had a special day for "turning out" each room, always cleaned the silver on Friday, and devoted Saturday to the kitchen. As for washing, I wished she had kept a special day for that, but she had a penchant for washing, and would wash at all hours. Things that seemed to be spotless would go into the tub if I turned my back ... I could see that Emma liked me to go out, so that she could get on with her work faster, and surprise me with her results on my return. ❞

AN ENGLISHMAN'S CASTLE **A typical middle-class English house surrounded by a garden gives the occupants privacy.**

a uniformly creditable character, and he is protected from the encroachments of manufacturing and other interests likely to include uncongenial neighbours. Saloons and shops, also, are excluded from these sacred precincts.' Zoning laws were enforced in order to keep out the 'influx of foreigners with low ideals of family life'.

For the middle classes, there was perhaps a weakening of the formerly strict boundaries between family life and society at large. Whereas previously, family activities such as eating meals together and entertaining guests had taken place largely at home, new habits of eating out, living in apartments, weekending with friends or holidaying abroad were now being adopted.

On the other hand, among lower-middle and affluent working-class families in Britain, Germany and North America, these boundaries strengthened, if anything, as more living space at home, often with a garden to work and play in, made home life more attractive. It was one of the marks of working-class life, for example, that even close friends were rarely invited into the home or to family meals.

British working-class families, in particular, rarely went out together to public places. A party of metalworkers from Birmingham, visiting Berlin in 1906, noted the Continental habit of living in flats, with the inevitable reduction in family privacy that this entailed, and observed that it was 'our self-contained cottages which make home sweet home a reality'. In France, and in the Mediterranean countries generally, on the other hand, home life still tended to spill out into the street outside the house and into the wider community of local shops, cafés and cheap eating places, where men and women met their friends.

There was a growing commitment to the idea of homemaking. Observers noted that English housewives were less skilled in cooking and the traditional household arts than their counterparts in France and Germany, but that their homes were more comfortable and clean; British and American families spent a higher proportion of their incomes on furniture and household goods than did their European counterparts.

Upward mobility could produce stress; there is evidence that child cruelty in Britain was more common in affluent working-class or lower middle-class families than among the poor. But the overwhelming impression from middle and affluent working-class memoirs of the time is of the home as a place of comfort, security and affectionate family relationships.

LOVE AND SEX

Despite the overall trend towards marrying later or not marrying at all, the marriage rate in areas where the employment of women was common was generally high and the marriage age low, presumably because the addition of a woman's wages made marriage more affordable. Divorce, in the United States and among the wealthier classes in Europe especially, occurred more frequently perhaps because people had higher emotional expectations of relationships.

In urban areas especially, there was a growing idea – which would accelerate rapidly

DANCING PARTNERS Modern dance styles were less formal than their predecessors, and allowed young couples a degree of physical contact.

FAMILY PLANNING

Throughout Europe, the birthrate declined between 1870 and 1914. In Britain in 1908, it was estimated that 79 per cent of the decline was due to 'deliberate restriction of childbearing', that is, contraception and abortion. There was great reluctance to discuss this subject, but by the 1890s postal retailing of contraceptives, advertised in magazines, was widespread. There is also evidence that among working-class women the practice of birth-control methods was virtually unknown.

---

in the 20th century – that marriage had to do with love and friendship rather than dynastic calculation or mutual economic support. Such a notion was strongly encouraged in the romantic love stories that were increasingly to be found in the magazines and novels of the time, and it also inevitably led to disappointed expectations and to marital breakdown.

The increasing divorce rate in the Anglo-Saxon countries was also sometimes linked with women's emancipation, particularly in North America. A University of Pennsylvania sociologist, writing in 1909, noted that a woman 'is not forced into marriage as her only means of support . . . If marriage is a failure, she does not face the alternatives of endurance or starvation. The way is open for independent support . . . She is no longer compelled to accept support or yield to the tyranny of a husband whose conduct is a menace to her health and happiness.' However, few European women in 1909 as yet had this kind of freedom of choice. Divorce in France, for example, was permitted only in cases where husband or wife was guilty of grave misconduct.

Victorian ideas about sexuality persisted, particularly the notion that respectable women were incapable of sexual enjoyment and endured sexual intercourse only as a matter of marital duty. There were undoubtedly large numbers of unhappy, unfulfilled marriages, and the prevalence of venereal disease indicates the extent to which men were still resorting to prostitutes – almost invariably young women from the lower classes for

JERSEY LILY The actress Lillie Langtry was one of the favourites of Edward, Prince of Wales.

whom the life offered better earnings than could be found in other occupations. Attempts to regulate prostitution had more to do with making it safer than with attempting to deal with its causes; men still widely held the view that prostitution was an essential safety valve in a world in which a man's natural urges could not be decently satisfied in his own home or among the women of his own group in society.

But there were some more modern undercurrents. A matrimonial handbook published in 1896 stated that: 'No observing person can doubt that the sexual relations of men and women determine in a great degree their happiness or misery.' And when an Anglican bishop suggested that sexual intercourse between married couples should be strictly confined to the purposes of procreation, it was Mrs Bramwell Booth, wife of the founder of the Salvation Army, who declared that: 'I have never heard such a view of married life entertained before.' A widely circulated American handbook stated that 'reciprocity in the sexual passion is indispensable to the contentment and happiness of the husband and wife'.

Official views apart, there is plentiful evidence that among at least a section of the upper classes, sexual morals were quite loose. It was a common practice, among the 'faster' social set, for bedrooms to be allocated during country-house weekends for the discreet conduct of adulterous affairs. Where marriages were based on dynastic considerations or economic calculation, it was accepted that love and physical passion would sometimes flow into different channels; the crime

LADIES OF THE NIGHT Prostitutes entertain a group of clients in a German brothel of the 1900s (left). Despite the respect for family life, such services were much in demand, and there were popular fears about women being sold into 'white slavery' (above).

was being found out. Edward VII, ruler of British, and to some extent of European, society was a noted exemplar of this principle, well-known for his attachments to mistresses who were themselves frequently married women. Equally, there were middle-class intellectuals, such as H.G. Wells, who were talking about, and openly practising, 'free love'. Nonetheless, an easier, happier attitude to sex within married life was probably the prevailing mood of the time.

Another factor influencing change in sexual morality was the increasing knowledge and availability of contraception methods, despite the hostility of the establishment and the Church. Contraceptives could be advertised, but only selectively – they were advertised massively in popular almanacs, for example, but not in national newspapers – and while they were not readily to be found in shops, they could be bought by post. Apart from sheaths and pessaries, other methods were available, from folk recipes, withdrawal and 'coughing after intercourse', to the most extreme form of birth-control – abortion.

GAY PARIS The French were more tolerant of homosexuality than were most European nations.

Homosexuality was probably as prevalent in 1900 as it is today, but male homosexual acts were a criminal offence in many countries and were regarded in most with abhorrence; love between men was, in the words of Oscar Wilde, 'the love that dare not speak its name'. Wilde himself caused a scandal that rocked society when in 1895, after suing the Marquess of Queensberry, father of his friend Lord Alfred Douglas, for calling him a 'sodomite', he was arrested for homosexual acts and sentenced to hard labour. His crime, in the eyes of sophisticated people at least, probably lay in allowing himself to be found out, instead of conducting his affairs discreetly. The reaction of the majority of people to the revelations at his trials, however, was rather that an age of innocence had come to an end and that a new age of unheard-of decadence and immorality had dawned.

In Germany during the 1900s, there was another scandal, with more serious implications, when Prince Philip von Eulenberg, an intimate friend of Kaiser Wilhelm II, was publicly accused of homosexuality. The charges against him were never conclusively proved. Nevertheless, the mere fact of the accusation, and the court cases that followed it, severely damaged the prestige of the German monarchy.

WOMEN AND WIVES

Most people, including most women, regarded a woman's proper role as that of homemaker

and mother, although employment opportunities for women were increasing, and women

were beginning to demand a more active role in public life.

A WOMAN'S WORLD   **Three generations of women entertain themselves in an English garden.**

THE SAME middle-class ideal of the woman's role that had developed during the 19th century persisted in most places at the beginning of the 20th; it had its roots in the economic and industrial change from cottage industry to factory production that had created a strict segregation of the spheres of work and home. Among middle-class families, the sexual division of labour was based, not on different roles in the running of an economic enterprise, as in older communities, but on supposedly 'natural' differences in the characters of the sexes. Women had been elevated to a pedestal of purity; they were the gentler sex, better at feeling than at thinking, more caring and selfless than men. They were ideally suited, therefore, to caring for the children and providing all the comforts of home for the men, who, for their part, were better fitted for the

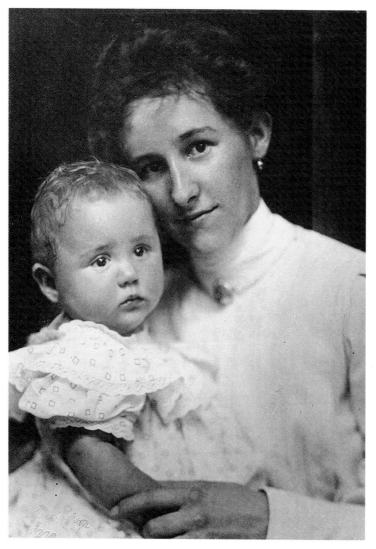

MOTHER AND CHILD   A photograph taken in 1906 epitomises the idealisation of the mother and child relationship, which was based on the view that motherhood was women's natural profession.

they were able to obtain some form of training for a professional career, this tended to be seen as an alternative to a woman's proper role as wife and mother – a fallback position for those who had, for one reason or another, failed to marry.

WORKING WOMEN

Many working-class women worked, but they did so mainly as domestic servants, or in laundries, shops, in the textile or garment-making industries, or in food-processing. Few earned wages that would have been high enough to keep them if they lived on their own. Most of them left work on marrying unless they were working in small family firms. In Berlin, for example, only 11 per cent of married women were in full-time employment in 1907.

In North America, on the other hand, women were joining the work-force on an unprecedented scale, and the sharpest increase was among young middle-class women, who were now taking on white-collar jobs, for example as secretaries, clerical workers and factory inspectors, that had previously been exclusively male. Far more than anywhere else, the North American business world was a place where men and women were working side by side – although women still tended to be limited to subordinate positions.

It was rare in middle-class European households for wives or daughters to contribute anything to the family income. The economic role of the middle-class wife was one of management – keeping accounts, directing servants, dealing with tradesmen, planning menus – and some middle-class women delegated even these tasks to their upper servants. All manual work was relegated to servants and to working-class women outside the home, and

rough work of the world. Women needed to be protected by men from the evil and corruption of the world. And since they were not naturally ambitious or equipped for analytic thought, there was no place for women in the public world of politics and business; consequently, there was no need for them to have any kind of higher education or professional training; motherhood itself was the highest and holiest of professions.

These views might have been largely imposed by men, but they were still held by the majority of women; even the feminists of the time tended to accept that a woman's primary role lay in the domestic sphere. As a result, few women had penetrated the professions by 1900, and then mostly as teachers. By 1914, there was still a long way for women to go in this respect. Even when

VOTES FOR WOMEN

New Zealand granted women the vote in 1893; Australia in 1902. Finland was the first country in Europe to enfranchise women, in 1906, followed by Norway in 1907; women in Germany, Austria, Britain and America had to wait much longer.

it was possible for a middle-class woman to have very few practical skills of any kind. Gwen Raverat, granddaughter of Charles Darwin, recalled that her mother 'would have told anyone how to do anything: the cook how to skin a rabbit, or the groom how to harness a horse; though of course she had never done, or even observed, these operations herself'.

In working-class homes, wives and children might make important, sometimes vital, contributions to the family income. In England alone, some 300 000 children were in regular employment in 1901, some working more than 40 hours a week, and their pay packets could raise a family from near-penury to relative affluence and comfort. Some of the less scrupulous factory owners calculated what was meant to be a living wage on the basis of a whole family's earnings, including those of children as young as ten.

In mining communities it was very rare for women to work, but in industries such as textiles and pottery it was common. Although some women might have worked for pin money or for the social opportunities of the factory, most undoubtedly did so to supplement a meagre male wage. Even when they were not regularly employed, many working-class women found ways of supplementing income; by childminding, taking in lodgers, dressmaking or charring.

Even when wives were not wage earners, they made a vital contribution to the household economy by acting as unpaid domestic labour, at a

WORKING WOMEN The majority of women who worked did so as domestic servants (top) or in family businesses, like these Paris delivery women.

THE LOWER DEPTHS Russian women and children look for coal near a worked-out mine.

time when that entailed an incessant round of cooking, cleaning, laundering, childcare, ironing, cleaning and polishing grates, laying fires and, for miners' wives, preparing the husband's daily bath. As aspirations and income rose in the late 19th century, housework grew more arduous, with more possessions to polish and dust, and higher standards of order and hygiene to maintain.

Perhaps most important of all, working-class women ran the household budget. Whether the husband handed over all or part of his wages, it was the wife who paid the bills, negotiated credit with shopkeepers, traded with the pawnbroker, put money away for clothes and holidays and – when times were bad – deprived herself in order to feed her husband and children.

THE DECLINE OF THE PATRIARCH

The mid-Victorian family had been strongly patriarchal, perhaps nowhere more so than in Britain. The British husband of the 1860s had an absolute right of control not only over his wife's property but of her person, too, as well as over their children. In disputes over custody, Victorian courts almost invariably upheld the rights of the father over those of the mother, however virtuous. In sexual matters, there was a profound inequality of legal rights. Adultery by a wife was automatic grounds for divorce, whereas adultery by a husband was regarded as an 'accident' and was not grounds for divorce unless accompanied by desertion or cruelty. A wife who left her husband's home could be forced to return to him by court order.

To some extent this was still true in the Edwardian era. A French observer, Emile Boutmy, noted in 1904 that 'up to our own days English family life has retained all the characteristics of an absolute monarchy', and went on to remark: 'I know of no person in the modern world who puts me more in mind of the ancient Roman paterfamilias than the head of an English family ... He is a monarch reverenced in his own kingdom, almost a monarch by divine right. Compared with him the [French head of a family] seems like a President

FATHERS AND SONS – DECLINE OF THE PATRIARCH

The British novelist and playwright Walter Greenwood recalls a friend of the family Dick Dacre, who had spent all his life working with horses, in conversation with his father. Dacre's son, Charlie, had had plans for a quite different career from that of his father:

❦ Instead of following his father's ancient trade Charlie was a votary of engineering to the point of infatuation. He was in the fourth year of his apprenticeship with a small engineering firm in Manchester whose principal, Mr Henry Royce, had, some years before, bought a French motor car. The performance of this had offended his fastidious sense of the right and proper. In consequence he had decided to make three new ones to his own design. It was to the development of this branch of the firm's trade that Charlie was utterly dedicated. Although he was genial, likable and had all else to commend him he was not my man. He smelled of oil, not provender, and perpetually his talk was of induction, compression, ignition and exhaust and, of course, his idol of idols, "Pa Royce". Between father and son existed a perpetual conflict of irreconcilables – horse versus machine.

"Well, Charlie," Father said, snipping away, "and how's the motor business?"

"Motor cars!" Dick Dacre said...

"Have it your own way, Dad," Charlie answered imperturbably. "Just tell me ... where're all your horse trams? Electric's taken over. What about Graham White? Flew over Buile Hill Park in his aeroplane. Look at the nobs on the Old Road. Cars, that's what they're going in for. Coachmen having to learn to be chauffeurs if they want to keep their jobs...."

"What d'you make of him, Tom?" Dick Dacre asked, despairingly.

"I dunno," Dad said. "They're noisy, stinking things, always breaking down."

"You've never heard o' the ones we make breaking down. Silver Ghost, London to Edinburgh and back in top gear all the way. What about that?"

His father snorted: "Too fast and too far." ❧

PATRIARCH The father of this French family (far left) stands in order to symbolise his role as protector and provider. But parents (left) were showing a new tenderness towards their children.

elected by a critical Parliament.' Boutmy was writing mainly about the families of the British landed gentry, where such old ways persisted; but in general, things had been changing. In Britain by the 1880s, a married woman had the legal right to hold, acquire and dispose of her own property and could have custody of the children when the courts deemed that this was conducive to their welfare. But as late as 1899, a British court could still uphold a man's right to rape his wife.

In truth, there were probably as many styles of family life in the years before the First World War as there were families. The traditional patriarchal family might linger on in European peasant communities and was still upheld as an ideal among the French and German bourgeoisie – the German Catholic Church, for example, fostered traditional authoritarian family values – but among younger people in urban society, at least, it was passing away.

At the same time, there was a decline, in the urban, industrial world, in the prestige and authority that had formerly attached to old age. Boutmy's notion of the stern Victorian paterfamilias, guardian and ruler of his family, was giving way, at least among younger middle-class people, to the idea of the husband as friend and companion to his wife and children.

The question of who was the 'head of the family' depended on social class, on occupation and on the personalities involved. In some areas and occupations – among miners, for example – a man would not dream of taking any part in domestic tasks and would have been ridiculed if he had; in others – for example among workers in the textile

industry – it was quite usual for men to share the work of childcare and household tasks.

Certainly there were many working-class families where there was no doubt that mother was the authority figure. The English observer Margaret Loan noted: 'I doubt if the bare idea of fathers being equal to mothers in authority even enters the mind of any cottage child under the age of sixteen. Father is generally regarded in the light of mother's eldest child, and disobedience in him is a far more heinous crime than in them, because "he'd ought to know better than not to do what mother says!" Fathers are as a rule perfectly satisfied with this position.'

The dominance of the mother in the realm of the home might be true even where, as in some French peasant communities, it was usual for her not to sit down to eat until she had fed her husband and children.

The decline of the idea of the father as moral and religious teacher and guardian of his family was linked with a decline in religious belief and moral certainty, and also with an increase in the

NEW WOMAN   A German woman student:
Germany was one of the last European countries
to admit women into universities. Inset: The New
Woman was the inspiration for a play written in
the 1890s by Sydney Grundy.

and sometimes even lending libraries and reading rooms. And for younger women, in particular, the fashion for bicycling offered the opportunity to go off by themselves, or even with male companions, unsupervised by a chaperone.

Women were still denied the vote almost everywhere, but from the 1880s on they were playing a greater part in both national and local politics. Nationally, they were prepared to campaign vigorously for male candidates for whom they could not vote. Locally, they were working actively in areas such as education, public health and sanitation. Upper middle-class women fought tirelessly for the rights of prostitutes, and gave evidence to public enquiries into sexually transmitted diseases.

While increasing affluence meant that many working-class wives could afford to withdraw from the labour market, increasing numbers of young middle-class women were actively seeking a way of life outside marriage in the form of higher education, professional training and social work. The provision of elementary education for children of both sexes, brought in by the Education Act of 1870 in England and in the early 1880s in France, stimulated this demand, and the need for teachers in the new elementary schools in itself offered thousands of young women the possibility of an independent life and of an occupation and professional status not available to them before.

Women reformers and intellectuals were beginning to challenge the assumptions of a male-dominated society: not just in their demands for the franchise and in their denunciation of the sexual double standard, but also in ways familiar today, in calling attention to the gendered structure of everyday language – the feminist writer Ellice Hopkins, for example, suggested that 'virtue'

general willingness on the part of men to hand over such responsibilities as these to their wives or to outside agents such as school-teachers and Sunday schools.

THE NEW WOMAN

Women at the dawn of the 20th century had far less freedom of movement than they were to have in the 1920s, but rather more than their mothers had. Department stores, for example, which had recently appeared in the larger cities, were places where respectable women could spend a large part of the day alone or with women friends; they were plentifully equipped with restaurants and tearooms, cloakrooms

EMANCIPATION   Young American women demonstrate their new freedom by wearing a masculine style of dress.

WOMEN'S RIGHTS Suffragettes march at the funeral of Emily Davison, who threw herself under King George V's horse at the 1913 Derby.

should be renamed *muliertude* (the state of being a woman) – and questioning the masculine characterisation of God in the scriptures.

Women seeking a role outside the home – or even simply more freedom within it – still went through a period of subterfuge and struggle. Even when, in the 1900s, they began to take up paid employment in public life – as doctors, nurses,

academics – they tended to specialise in the areas deemed suitable for women, and many compensated for the fact that they were working at all by emphasising supposedly feminine characteristics such as modesty and propriety.

The dominant view, held by many women as well as by men, was still that a woman's place was in the home; and it was still scientifically orthodox

to assume that women's minds were inferior and that, for example, prolonged education or mental effort of any kind were deleterious to a woman's reproductive processes and her mental health. Although education was becoming more available to women, gender divisions in education were, if anything, more pronounced than ever. As a British educationist put it in 1911, boys should be instructed in 'courage, self-control, hard work, endurance and protection of the weak', while girls should be taught 'gentleness, care for the young and helpless, interest in domestic affairs, and admiration for the strong and manly character in men'.

EYEWITNESS

A SUFFRAGETTE SUFFERS FOR THE CAUSE

The suffragette Lady Constance Lytton was in jail in 1910, having disguised herself as a working-class woman so that she would not receive privileged treatment. On the fourth day of her hunger strike, the prison medical officer declared that she must be made to eat:

❛ He urged me to take food voluntarily. I told him that was absolutely out of the question, that when our legislators ceased to resist enfranchising women then I should cease to resist taking food in prison ... I offered no resistance to being placed in position, but lay down voluntarily on the plank bed. Two of the wardresses took hold of my arms, one held my head and one my feet ... The doctor leant on my knees as he stooped over my chest to get at my mouth. I shut my mouth and clenched my teeth. I had looked forward to this moment with so much anxiety lest my identity should be discovered beforehand, that I felt positively glad when the time had come ...

FORCED FEEDING **A suffragette propaganda poster is aimed at persuading women to vote against the Government.**

The doctor offered me the choice of a wooden or steel gag; he explained elaborately, as he did on most subsequent occasions, that the steel gag would hurt and the wooden one not, and he urged me not to force him to use the steel gag. But I did not speak nor open my mouth, so that after playing about for a moment or two with the wooden one he finally had recourse to the steel. He seemed

annoyed at my resistance and he broke into a temper as he plied my teeth with the steel implement ... He said if I resisted so much with my teeth, he would have to feed me through the nose. The pain of it was intense and at last I must have given way for he got the gag between my teeth, when he proceeded to turn it much more than necessary until my jaws were fastened wide apart, far more than they could go naturally. Then he put down my throat a tube which seemed to me much too wide and was something like 4 ft [1.2 m] in length. The irritation of the tube was excessive. I choked the moment it touched my throat until it had got down. Then the food was poured in quickly; it made me sick a few seconds after it was down and the action of the sickness made my body and legs double up, but the wardresses instantly pressed back my head and the doctor leant on my knees. The horror of it was more than I can describe. ❜

THE WORLD OF CHILDREN

A general relaxation in family relationships, the introduction of compulsory elementary education for all, and new theories on childcare that emphasised the importance of play and leisure in children's development, initiated an extended and more carefree childhood for many children.

FOR THE CHILDREN of the comfortably off, the years around the beginning of the 20th century were a good time to be alive. In the mid 19th century, childhood had effectively ended by the age of ten, if not before, for most children. By the end of the century, however, compulsory elementary education, coupled with restrictions on children's employment, meant that childhood was becoming longer for children of the working class.

In Europe and North America, families in general were gradually becoming smaller, with an average of three or four children against the five or more of mid-Victorian times. In Britain, for example, by the 1900s only the wives of miners and quarrymen were producing families as large as those of the mid-Victorian period; these were trades and communities in which women traditionally did not work outside the home (in the textile industry, where female employment was high, birthrates were lower). The reasons for this reduction in average family size are uncertain, but may well have had something to do with the fact that middle-class people were becoming more conscious of the cost of educating children. Furthermore, compulsory state education was taking children out of the labour market and thus turning them into financial liabilities rather than assets for the family.

Whatever the reason, smaller families meant that parents could invest more time and emotion in

THE HAPPIEST DAYS Children play in a Paris park in 1905. Play and exercise were regarded as important aspects of a child's development.

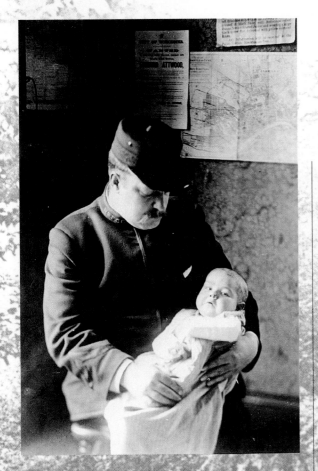

SUFFER THE CHILDREN An officer of the National Society for the Prevention of Cruelty to Children tends one of the Society's young charges.

discipline, health and education in the home, and about such matters as infant feeding and toilet training. There was also a growing conviction in most of the countries of Western Europe and North America that child-rearing was not just a private matter; mothers had more than a private responsibility for their own children – they were responsible for the future of the race.

The law, and society at large, were beginning to intervene in family life, mainly to protect the rights of children. The National Society for the Prevention of Cruelty to Children (NSPCC) was set up in Britain in the 1880s, and similar societies were formed soon afterwards in North America and other European countries; Britain and the United States led the way in legislation prohibiting cruelty to children, and in the 1900s in Britain a Children's Charter laid down in detail the duties of parents in matters such as care and maintenance, medical attention, abstention from tobacco and alcohol, exclusion of children from public houses, and prevention of injuries and burns. In 1900 the

the rearing of their children. From the 1890s on, there was a flood of publications about child development and the importance of exercise, fresh air and play, and new ideas circulated about

International Association for Labour Legislation, with members in most advanced countries, was established in Switzerland to promote, among other things, the regulation, although not the abolition, of child labour. Elementary schooling was compulsory in the countries of Western Europe and North America.

DISCOVERING THE WORLD OF CHILDHOOD

In Britain – and to a much lesser extent in other countries – thousands of middle-class children, boys in particular, were sent away to boarding school, but for middle-class children at home there were rapidly rising standards of physical and material care. A middle-class mother could excel at and enjoy motherhood as never before. Parent-child relationships were becoming easier,

DOTING PARENTS   A young couple gaze lovingly at their new baby in this American postcard of 1911.

friendlier and less strict and formal. By the 1890s, traditionalists were even complaining about the practice of children addressing their mothers by Christian names or nicknames.

The attitude to children was changing. The early Victorians, however much they may have sentimentalised childhood in general, believed that it was a time of depravity (due to their notions about original sin – that everyone is born in a state of moral weakness, against which they must continually fight), when only strict punishment and discipline could keep children on the road to salvation; 'Spare the rod and spoil the child' was a proverb that summed up this attitude. 'Play' was limited and was almost invariably given an educational or moral dimension.

Such attitudes persisted at the end of the century in the institutions, such as workhouses and orphanages, where many of the children of the poor still lived, and in British boarding schools, but in general a happier, freer attitude was beginning to prevail. Children could be cherished and enjoyed, and, just as importantly, they could be allowed, and even encouraged, to enjoy themselves. 'Up to now the world of childhood has been an undiscovered or at least an unexplored land', an English paediatrician wrote in 1910. 'The child is a new discovery.'

Although there was no question of sexual permissiveness, for example, middle-class parents began to think it a good thing to teach their children about the 'facts of life'. Reasoning began to replace corporal punishment; rather than being told to keep silent in the presence of adults – 'Children should be seen and not heard' was another familiar Victorian proverb – children were encouraged to learn the art of conversation. The old-fashioned view that their natural wickedness must be constantly kept in check was giving way to a greater tendency to consider their feelings, not least their capacity for boredom; efforts were made to keep them amused and entertained as well as educated and morally instructed. Children were taken out by their parents on excursions and expeditions – to the zoo, to the theatre, on picnics, and to the

MOTHER'S HELP In poor families, the older children were often left to bring up their younger brothers and sisters (above). In well-to-do families, however, the children were generally brought up by servants (right).

seaside – as they only rarely had been earlier in the 19th century.

Of course there were cases of parental neglect. There were upper-class mothers who left their children to be brought up by servants – Winston Churchill's schoolboy letters are full of poignant appeals to an adored mother who seemed to want to have very little to do with him – and there were some among working-class mothers who left their children to 'bring up themselves', or who tranquillised their children with alcohol or opium-based cordials.

There were also mothers who, for reasons of chronic ill-health, poverty and an unhealthy environment, simply could not cope. Towelling nappies, for example, came on the market in the 1890s, but were beyond the means of poorer women, who in any case had no access to the constant supplies of hot water needed to keep them clean. Yet records of the time show working-class women

PING-PONG

Table tennis was invented around 1889 by a British engineer, James Gibb, who first played it on his dining-room table using cigar-box lids as bats and balls made from champagne corks. Later, he had Celluloid balls made in the United States. In 1898 he had sets marketed under the name 'Gossima'. When Jaques changed the name to Ping-Pong, it caught on rapidly and swept Britain and the United States in the early 1900s. The first table-tennis bat with a studded rubber surface appeared in 1902.

Toys for the Boys, Dolls for the Girls

Ernest Shepard, illustrator of *Winnie the Pooh* and the other children's classics written by A.A. Milne, as well as of *The Wind in the Willows* by Kenneth Grahame, was brought up in London at the end of the 19th century, the child of successful and prosperous middle-class parents.

His memoirs provide an enchanting evocation of late-Victorian childhood at its happiest and most secure.

6 Cyril and I spent much time in the playroom, reviewing our armies of toy soldiers and fighting pitched battles on the floor. Father had made us a "river" for our pontoon train; it was of painted cardboard with two "banks" of green baize and was most realistic. Slots were cut for the little boats to sit in, so that we could build a complete bridge across. Our little blue-uniformed soldiers with the spiked helmets made light work of storming across, regardless of the hail of rifle fire from the opposite bank. Disputes always arose as to the number of casualties incurred, and I fear that we never solved any tactical problems. Always it happened that either a meal was announced or it was time to go to bed – and a very good way of settling a war too!

We unearthed Ethel's doll's house from the loft. This had once been a source of great joy to us. We had helped Ethel to arrange and rearrange the furniture and to see to the comfort of the inhabitants. But this was before the advent of the toy soldier age. We now carried the house downstairs and set it up on the playroom table. Then we proceeded to take stock. It had been put away for some years so that things were in disorder. But Cyril and I got busy and did some extensive repair work. We made quite a number of useful additions, and, by using the forbidden modelling wax discreetly, we found that things could be kept in place: the members of the family in residence, for example, could be fixed to their chairs with dollops of wax on the seats, and thus the wretched creatures (a few china dolls) were condemned to sit at rigid attention instead of sliding off onto the floor. We tried to make a table-lamp with a real nightlight inside, but the result was too big to go on the table and it fell off, setting alight some lace curtains. The doll's house was then banished back to the loft. 9

struggling in adverse circumstances not merely to keep their children clean, healthy and regularly fed, but also to teach them ideas about privacy, modesty and good manners.

For Amusement Only

Children's clothes, games, books and toys all reflected this new attitude and, as these products were increasingly being mass produced, they were reaching an ever-widening market. Small boys were put into knickerbockers, or jumpers and shorts, or sailor suits, rather than the 'petticoats' of earlier days. The older children of the comfortably off were given their own bedrooms rather than sleeping in communal nurseries. There were new fashions in entertainment produced specifically for children, such as the English pantomime (formerly a low form of entertainment) and plays written for children, such as *Peter Pan* (1904) and *Where the Rainbow Ends* (1910).

The last decades of the 19th century were the first era in which books and games began to be produced for the undiluted pleasure of children

PARADISE An American boy gazes at the wonderful contents of a toy store. Toys had come to be regarded as an important part of learning as well as amusement for children.

GOLDEN DAYS Seaside holidays were one of the joys of an Edwardian childhood.

THE CHRISTMAS BUSINESS A thoroughly modern Father Christmas arrives for work by motor car.

Boys' toys ranged from marbles and the simple iron hoop, often made by the local blacksmith, to superbly carved and painted hobbyhorses, clockwork model trains, toy soldiers (often made in Germany), and the first Meccano construction sets.

The practice of giving children toys, dolls and games culminated at Christmas, which was now more than ever seen as a festival of gift-giving, when the great department stores, for example, opened special Christmas toy bazaars and inaugurated the custom of employing a man to dress as Father Christmas.

The 1880s, the 1890s and the 1900s were a golden age for children's literature, particularly in the Anglo-Saxon countries, producing in Britain, for example, Oscar Wilde's *The Happy Prince*, the novels of Robert Louis Stevenson, such as *Treasure Island*, E. Nesbit's *Five Children and It* and *The Railway Children*, tales such as *The Jungle Books* and *Kim* by Rudyard Kipling, the incomparable stories and illustrated work of Beatrix Potter, and Kenneth Grahame's *The Wind in the Willows*; in the United States, L. Frank Baum's *The Wonderful Wizard of Oz* and the novels of Frances Hodgson Burnett (*A Little Princess, Little Lord Fauntleroy,* and *The Secret Garden*); and in Germany, the hugely popular Wild West tales of Karl May.

Paradoxically, as the Victorian ideas of discipline, silence at meals and reticence about sex faded among the middle class, they probably grew stronger among the respectable working class. At the same time, the more affluent working-class parents strove to give

rather than as a sweetener for moral instruction. Board games, which were often beautifully printed in colour, were popular with both boys and girls, but toys still generally reflected traditional views of male and female roles. Girls had dolls, now realistically modelled, that could be elaborately dressed, and doll's houses in which to accommodate them.

CHILDREN'S CHOICE In his Wild West adventure stories, Karl May achieved a remarkable degree of realistic detail, although he never left his native Germany. Right: Peter Rabbit, one of Beatrix Potter's most popular characters, made his first appearance in 1900.

TEDDY: THE STORY OF A BEAR

SOFT TOYS for children began to appear in the 1800s. By far the most enduring of them has been the Teddy Bear, which made its first appearance around 1902.

In that year, a Washington newspaper carried a cartoon showing the then President of the United States, Theodore 'Teddy' Roosevelt, refusing to shoot a captive bear cub. The cartoon conveyed a political message, but the public were more struck by the engaging drawing of the cuddly little bear, and the drawing was reproduced in several other newspapers.

The story goes that it was noticed by a Russian immigrant named Morris Mitchom, who ran a sweetshop in Brooklyn where he also sold toys, some of them made by Mitchom himself and his wife. Mitchom decided to make and sell a toy based on the newspaper drawing, made out of a deep-pile fabric called plush to imitate the bear's furry coat, and with movable arms and legs. He displayed it in the window of his shop next to a cutting from the newspaper and labelled it 'Teddy's Bear'.

Mitchom's son later claimed that his father had written to the president asking permission to use his name in this way, and that he received a handwritten reply as follows: 'I don't think my name is worth much to the toy bear cub business, but you are welcome to use it.'

This document was not discovered among Morris Mitchom's papers at his death, but what is certain is that in 1903 the firm of Bulter Bros took Mitchom's entire stock, thus guaranteeing his credit with the fabric suppliers. The new business was called the Ideal Novelty and Toy Company; it is now the Ideal Toy Co, the biggest doll manufacturer in the world.

However, there is another claimant to the ancestry of the Teddy Bear. Since 1880 in Germany, the Steiff Company had been manufacturing a wide range of soft animal toys. In 1902 the proprietor's nephew produced a design for a plush bear cut with movable limbs and head.

The new toy was not well received in the German toy trade at first, but in 1903, it is claimed, an American firm ordered 3000 units. However the bear may have been named, the Steiff company

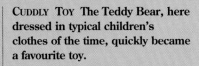

CUDDLY TOY The Teddy Bear, here dressed in typical children's clothes of the time, quickly became a favourite toy.

were certainly one of the first manufacturers.

The name 'Teddy Bear' appeared in print for the first time in 1906, by which time the bears had become a craze, being used, for example, as car mascots. By 1914 they were well established as much-loved children's toys. It is virtually certain, however, that they were named after 'Teddy' Roosevelt.

The oldest surviving British-owned Teddy Bear is a Steiff bear, which was recorded as being bought in Edinburgh in 1903.

their children the comfort, the pleasures and the moral security of a happy home. Separate bedrooms might not always be affordable, but most parents endeavoured to give their children as much privacy as was possible. In addition, rising incomes meant that holidays, specially made children's clothes (rather than adult cut-downs) and toys could be afforded.

There were still aristocratic, and perhaps also some working-class, fathers who did not know the names of their own children, but in middle-class and prosperous working-class homes there was a new feeling of intimacy, friendship and mutual confidence between parents and children. There was the sense that childhood was a special time, to be nurtured and treasured.

FOOD AND DIET

While the middle classes and those living in rural areas could use specialist shops and markets supplied

with local produce, the increasing number of city-dwellers were catered for by the new multiple

grocery stores, which offered a wide range of packaged and branded goods at competitive prices.

FESTIVE FARE A prosperous working-class family enjoys a well-laden table at Christmas. Left: A London street urchin, on the other hand, relies on the Salvation Army for his farthing breakfast.

A T THE TURN of the century, the range of diet in the countries of the Western world could scarcely have been wider. For a middle-class family living in one of the cities of Britain and North America, it might well include canned, packaged and branded foods, including brands familiar today such as Heinz, Crosse and Blackwell, Nestlé, Quaker Oats and Shredded Wheat; the peasantry of continental Europe, on the other hand, still lived very largely on what they grew themselves or what was grown by their neighbours and sold in local markets.

At the lowest end of the social scale, it was still possible to die of starvation. In London in 1890, to take only one example from many, Salvation Army workers saw a man collapse in St James's Park; he died soon afterwards in hospital, where it was found that he had walked from Liverpool and had not eaten for five days. At the top of the scale, people dined less heavily than the mid-Victorians, but with a magnificence and variety of food and drink that had never been seen before.

SOAP AND MARGARINE

By 1900 the chemical process of combining hydrogen with a wide variety of substances to produce 'hardened' fats had been perfected. Two important results of this were the large-scale, low-cost production of soap, hitherto an expensive luxury, and margarine. Whale oil and a variety of cheap vegetable oils were the basis of a booming soap industry, supported by massive popular advertising, which brought personal cleansing products within the means of the poorer classes for the first time. Margarine offered the working classes a cheap and palatable alternative to butter, although the earlier margarines, which contained beef fat, were more nutritious than the later ones, which were made entirely of vegetable oils. Danes had the highest per capita consumption of margarine because Denmark exported its dairy products to the rest of Europe. Soap and margarine stimulated the growth of some huge international companies before the First World War: Lever Brothers in Britain, Procter & Gamble in the United States, and Van den Bergh in Holland.

Starvation apart, the poorest diet in Europe as a whole was probably that of the urban poor in Britain, many of whom lived on bread, margarine and tea, and very little else. Moreover, bread was now produced by roller-milling, so that, although white bread could be produced cheaply, it lacked both bran and wheatgerm, its most nutritious elements; the milk drunk in tea was often condensed skimmed milk.

A poorly paid working man living on bread, margarine and sweet tea, therefore, was less well nourished than his forefathers who, though even poorer in money terms, had lived on stone-ground bread, butter and beer. And since the man of the family must keep up his strength for his work, his wife and children might fare even worse. One researcher in a Lancashire town noted that: 'A treat for the smallest child consisted of a round of bread lightly sprinkled with sugar – the "sugar butty". But such was the craving for sweetness among the most deprived, some children I have known would take leaves from the bottom of their father's pot and spread them over bread to make the "sweet tea-leaf sandwich".'

Provided that he had good wages and competitive shops nearby, the British working man benefited from cheap food, with bread at 6d for a 4 lb (1.8 kg) loaf, potatoes at $^{1}/_{2}$d per lb (450 g), cheese at 8d per lb, tea at 1s 6d and sugar at 2d per lb, and imported beef and mutton at around 5d per lb. This was due to the British policy of Free Trade (a policy not pursued elsewhere in Europe at this time), which allowed huge imports of wheat from Canada and India, meat from the United States, Argentina, Germany, Australia and New Zealand, and bacon and dairy produce from Denmark. The first successful cargo of frozen beef and mutton had been brought from Melbourne to London in 1880; soon afterwards, pork from the United States, beef from the Argentine and lamb from New Zealand were pouring into the British market, making meat affordable for the poorer classes.

The lowest-paid British agricultural labourer, though he might add bacon and cheese

COLOURFUL CONTAINERS Foodstuffs were increasingly being packaged and branded.

GETTING AWAY FROM IT ALL Family picnics in the park – with their associations with a leisurely lifestyle and life in the countryside – were a favourite recreation for French town-dwellers.

to his diet, was scarcely better off than the poorest town workers: although he worked on the land, he only rarely ate fresh meat, milk and eggs, and there was plentiful evidence of dietary deficiency among the rural population. That both the urban and the rural population were often seriously undernourished came to light during the South African War of 1899-1902, when the Inspector General of Army Recruiting noted that 37.6 per cent of volunteers had been found unfit for service or were shortly afterwards invalided out.

Although wages in continental Europe were substantially lower on average than in Britain, the diet of the poor in those countries was rather healthier. Even the biggest European cities had not lost their connections with the countryside, where most people still had relatives, and regular supplies of fresh produce were still brought to the urban markets. For the same reason, the food of ordinary people in Europe was still strongly regional in character. On the whole, food production in continental Europe was as yet less industrialised than it had become in Britain and North America, and although working people might have to spend a very high percentage of their income on food, at the expense of clothing or furnishings for their homes, the food available to them was more varied and nutritious.

Continental Europeans also enjoyed the benefit

THE FISH-AND-CHIP SHOP

THANKS TO the development of the deep-sea steam trawler, and the possibility of packing fish in ice and transporting it by rail, the supply of wet fish to British towns increased hugely in the last decades of the 19th century.

The rise of the British fish-and-chip shop coincided with supplies of cheap cod and, probably, with the availability of vegetable fats and oils. The date at which the

deep-fried chipped potato, a French invention, was added to the fish is not known for certain, but Lancashire claims to be the birthplace of the combination of fish and chips. There were estimated to be 25 000 fish-and-chip shops in Britain by 1914. They catered almost exclusively to the working classes and made an important contribution to the protein content of the urban diet.

FISH SUPPER Fish and chips offered cheap nutrition for the poorer classes in Britain.

INFORMAL DINING   A Canadian couple allow their cat to share their dining table.

of a multitude of small, family-run restaurants that provided very much the same dishes as people were used to eating at their own tables, and in which people could eat for very little more than the cost of meals at home.

When continental European working-class families patronised restaurants, they brought to them a knowledge of how traditional dishes should be made, and of good wine and cheese, that the British proletariat had either never had or had lost

FIFTY-SEVEN VARIETIES

The tomato ketchup of the American food manufacturer H.J. Heinz was sold at London's Fortnum and Mason from 1886 along with other Heinz products. Heinz baked beans were introduced in the United States in 1895. In 1905-6 they were piloted in the North of England, where, surprisingly, they met 'no immediate response'.

after a century of massive urbanisation and industrialisation. Eating outside the home, other than at the fish-and-chip shop, was still unusual for British working-class people. Only at the very end of the 19th century did chains of inexpensive eating places, such as those of Joseph Lyons and the Aerated Bread Company, begin to appear, and these catered mainly to office workers and shoppers up from the suburbs.

Meanwhile, North Americans, Australians, New Zealanders and white South Africans, with a diet rich in meat and dairy produce, were probably the most generously nourished people in the world, by 1900 markedly taller and more robust on average than their European counterparts.

HAUTE CUISINE

By the end of the 19th century, France was everywhere acknowledged as the leader of the Western world in matters of cuisine. The great hotels, restaurants and private houses, whether in Paris, New York, Berlin or London, felt bound to employ a French chef, or at the very least a chef trained and practised in the French tradition. Menus were written in French, and classic French dishes were served. Port, sherry, Madeira, Hungarian Tokay and German dessert wines might be served after dinner, but the table wines were almost invariably French. Champagne was the favourite wine of the day among the wealthy and fashionable, and was sometimes drunk with every course from soup through to cheese and dessert.

The following is a typical dinner menu of the early 1900s. Something like it might have been served in a very grand restaurant or a wealthy household in Brussels or Berlin, New York or Melbourne, but it was in fact cooked for a dinner (an everyday dinner, not a special occasion) at the court of King Edward VII at Buckingham Palace on June 4, 1902:

Turtle Punch	*Turtle soup*
Madeira, 1816	*Cold consommé*
Johannesburg, 1868	*Whitebait au Naturel and à la Diable*
	Cold fillets of trout à la Norvegienne
Magnums Moet et Chandon, 1884	*Chicken wings à la Diplomate*
	Warm quails à la Russe
Chambertin, 1875	*Haunch of Sandringham venison, sauce aigre-doux*
	Cold saddle of lamb à l'Andalouse

Still Sillery, 1865	*Ortolans sur Canapés*
	Salad à la Bagration
Chateau Latour, 1875	*Asparagus d'Argenteuil*
	Peaches à la Reine Alexandre
	Patisserie Parisienne
	Cassolettes à la Jockey Club
	Trolley of assorted ice creams
	Wafers

Royal Tawny Port
Royal White Port
Sherry, Geo. IV
Chateau Margaux, 1871
Brandy, 1800

Edward VII's mother, Queen Victoria, had preferred plain food for herself – her breakfast was a boiled egg, served in a gold egg cup and eaten with a gold spoon – but she insisted that her table should be magnificent, as befitted an imperial monarch. On every day of the year at her court, Indian servants prepared curries in the royal kitchens in case they should be required by visitors from the Orient.

Towards the end of her reign, she employed a kitchen staff of 45, presided over by the Royal Chef, a Frenchman naturally, M. Menager, who received the large salary of £400 per annum, lived in his own house, and came to work in the morning in a hansom cab. On ordinary occasions, he worked with 18 other chefs, but for banquets like the one given for the Queen's Diamond Jubilee in 1897, as many as 24 extra French chefs were engaged, since each of the 14 courses took several days to prepare.

Edward VII himself was a noted trencherman, who would start a typical day with a breakfast of haddock, poached eggs, bacon, chicken and cold game, and still be ready for 12 courses at luncheon

---

TAKE A POWDER

Aspirin in a form pure enough to be used therapeutically was developed by Dr Felix Hoffman of Bayer AG and introduced commercially by Bayer in 1899. Available on prescription, it was produced only in powder form until 1915. Bayer aspirin was imported into Britain from 1905 until 1914, when manufacture was taken over by a British company.

HAUTE CUISINE As eating out became popular, hotel restaurants reached new heights of splendour. French chefs (inset) were much sought after by restaurants and private houses.

MARKETING **French people still did their daily shopping in open markets that were often supplied by local producers, but advertising (left) was stimulating demand for branded goods.**

and dinner. When he was at the races or the opera, footmen went ahead equipped with table linen, silver and gold plate, and hampers laden with cold dishes. A supper in the king's private room behind his box at Covent Garden might well consist of cold consommé, lobster mayonnaise, cold trout, duck, lamb cutlets, plovers' eggs, chicken, tongue and jellied ham, assorted sandwiches, strawberries and other fresh fruit, ending with French patisseries. (Plovers' eggs, incidentally, were an especially expensive luxury, costing 2s 6d each – the daily wage of an agricultural labourer in the 1900s.)

In this respect, however, King Edward, who was known as the First Gentleman of Europe, was a model for the aristocracy and the very rich everywhere. Although some of the calorific content of these enormous meals was worked off on the hunting field or the tennis court, it is not surprising that well-to-do males, in particular, had to go from time to time to the spas of France and Germany in order to rest and restore their livers and to try to lose a little weight.

Of course these lavish luncheons and dinners were not consumed in full; fashionable women with an eye to their figures only picked at each dish. The servants no doubt took their share of what was left over, but the waste was still, to some people, shocking. General Booth, founder of the Salvation Army, noted that: 'Sometimes legs of mutton from which only one or two slices had been cut were thrown into the tub . . . It is by no means an excessive estimate to assume that the waste out of the kitchens of the West End would provide a sufficient sustenance for all the Out-of-Work who will be employed in our labour sheds.' General Booth himself, and other philanthropists, set up Household Salvage Brigades to collect such wasted food and distribute it to the poor.

SHOPPING FOR FOOD

Most continental Europeans bought their food from local shops specialising as butchers, bakers, *patissiers*, *traiteurs*, delicatessens and so forth, or from open markets to which local farmers brought their produce. In the United States, multiple food retailing originated with the Great Atlantic & Pacific Tea Company in 1864. However, because of the vast scale of the country, the market there remained relatively undeveloped. It was in Britain that multiple grocery chains were most highly developed by the beginning of the 20th century.

The earliest multiple grocery stores in Britain were the branches of the Co-operative Wholesale Society, which had been pioneered in Rochdale in 1844. Its principle was to buy wholesale in bulk so as to obtain the best prices, to sell only for cash, and to divide the profits among members at the end of each year. By the year 1914

CRAFTSMAN The butcher, like the baker and the grocer, served an apprenticeship in his skilled craft.

CO-OP A Co-operative Wholesale Society store opens in London in around 1900.

there were 3 800 000 members of cooperative societies in Britain; these stores, now often selling coal, clothing and furniture as well as groceries, had a combined annual turnover of more than £100 000 000 and were paying out dividends as high as 2s 6d in the pound.

The practice of buying a limited range of goods in bulk and selling them at competitive prices was increasingly adopted at the end of the 19th century by pioneers who recognised that working-class spending power, though individually modest, was collectively enormous. Thomas Lipton, for example, with grocery stores in most major English cities, began in 1889 to sell tea at 1s 7d per lb (450 g) – up until then the minimum price had been 2s 6d per lb (450 g). His success was enormous; by 1914 he had 500 shops and a knighthood, and could afford to race yachts and entertain royalty.

On similar lines, the Maypole Dairy Company, established in 1898, sold only butter, margarine, tea and condensed milk – major ingredients of the

MARKS AND SPENCER

Michael Marks and Tom Spencer opened their Penny Bazaar in Manchester in 1894. Marks started business with a loan of £5, first as a pedlar, then as a street trader. Spencer provided the finance for the first Penny Bazaar; by 1900 there were 12, and by 1915 there were 140 throughout Britain.

DESIGNER CHEESE Many of the packaging designs of the 1890s and 1900s – a result of the increasing variety and choice of foods – are still in use today.

British working-class diet. Home and Colonial Stores, offering a wider range of groceries, had 400 branches by 1914. Sainsbury's, catering to a more middle-class clientele, had 115 branches, still mainly in the Greater London area, by 1914. In all, 114 grocery firms owned 2870 branches between them in 1910, many of them open from 7 am until 10 or 11 pm; and 23 meat companies controlled 3828 butchers' shops. In a similar way, brewery companies owned more than 75 per cent of all the licensed public houses in Britain.

In no other country was the retailing of food and drink concentrated in so few hands. On the whole, however, the chains catered to the less well-off. Middle-class people could still rely on deferential local shopkeepers, quite accustomed to dealing on account and to delivering meat, vegetables and groceries, increasingly ordered by telephone, to customers' homes. The grocer's van, the horse-drawn milk-cart and the butcher's boy on his bicycle were all familiar sights in middle-class residential areas.

The range of foodstuffs available from the grocer grew ever wider, as a young wife of the 1890s recalled: 'About this time, factory-prepared foods, soups and sauces came into greater use: jams, jellies, potted meats, tinned and bottled fruits, also labour-saving foods such as ready-cut lump sugar and "castor" sugar, stoned raisins, pounded almonds, prepared and chopped suet in packets, packet jellies, powdered gelatin, and all sorts of patent cleansers. Fewer and fewer people baked at home, except in the north.'

But although such packaged foods were increasingly available, many were still sold loose from bulk. Grocers were still apprenticed to a skilled trade, in which cheese was cut and cold meats sliced at the counter, and goods such as sugar, flour and tea were measured out of their containers and neatly wrapped in brown paper. The grocer's shop of the 1890s was still redolent of a hundred different enticing smells.

AT YOUR SERVICE Middle-class people could expect most of their food – which they often ordered over the telephone – to be delivered.

MIND, BODY AND SPIRIT

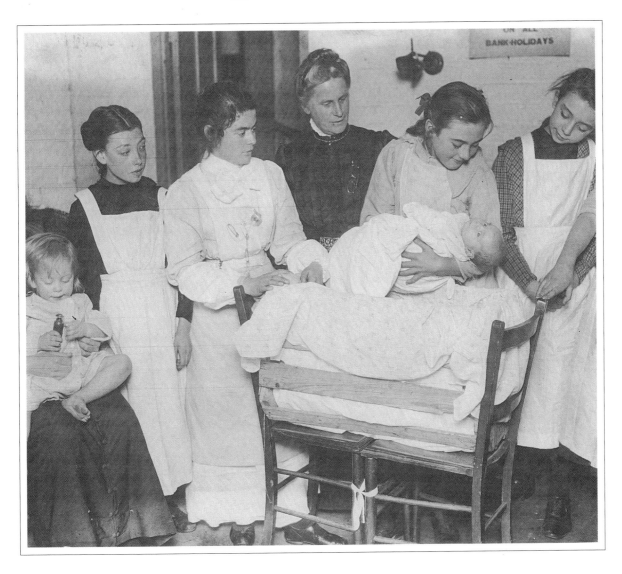

By 1900 there was free elementary education for all in the countries of Europe and North America. Secondary education, however, was only available to the privileged few. Improvements in general health were due at least as much to improved public hygiene and health education as to medical advances. Orthodox religious belief and church attendances both declined, but the religious impulse was channelled into strange new forms.

SCHOOLS FOR RICH AND POOR

Literacy rates soared in the industrialised countries as children from all backgrounds

began to attend school, but only the wealthy or the especially gifted

could expect a university education.

BY 1900 most countries in the industrialised world had a national system of free and compulsory elementary education. This had developed because of rapidly increasing industrialisation and an extension of the political franchise, leading to the recognition that it was desirable to have an educated work force and literate voters. One consequence was that illiteracy was virtually eliminated in the countries of northern and western Europe, North America, Australia and New Zealand. Elsewhere in Europe the situation was more patchy: in Italy, for example, the illiteracy rate in Piedmont, in the north, in 1901 was 17 per cent but in Calabria, in the south, nearly 80 per cent.

However, mass elementary education also had an indirect but important social effect in that it offered thousands of educated young women the chance of a job outside the home, freeing them from economic dependence on parents or husbands and enabling them, if they chose, to leave home altogether and rent their own accommodation,

AN EXCEPTIONAL STUDENT

In 1904, at the age of 24, Helen Keller graduated *cum laude* from Radcliffe College, Cambridge, Massachusetts, as a qualified doctor. Yet she had been born blind, deaf and mute. Unable to communicate, she had also been thought to be severely disturbed, but in 1887 she came into the hands of an inspired and dedicated teacher, Anne Sullivan, who taught her to read, write and speak. Keller published *The Story of My Life* in 1902.

something almost unheard of earlier in the 19th century.

Education was very formal and strictly disciplined. In the German-speaking world, girls and boys were taught in separate elementary schools wherever possible; in other countries, schools were generally co-educational, but boys and girls were segregated in the playground and in the classroom. This had less to do with fears about immoral behaviour resulting from a mixing of the sexes than with an assumption that boys and girls had different educational needs. Once they had acquired the basic skills of reading, writing and arithmetic, and some elementary history and geography, the curriculum diverged into subjects thought suitable for boys, such as training in woodwork and metalwork, and those thought

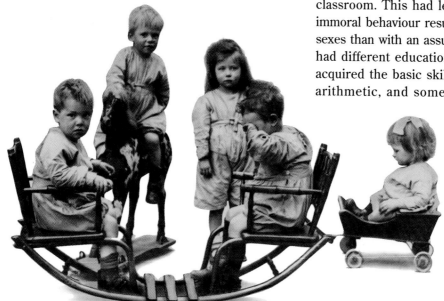

PLAYTIME Crèches for the children of working mothers were still rare in the years before the First World War.

WIFELY DUTIES In a German school in 1908, girls are instructed in the virtues of a woman's place: Church, kitchen and children.

state education system. However, in France, private schools providing basic religious teaching were permitted, and one in five children of primary-school age attended such schools. In Germany and in Britain, on the other hand, religious instruction was a compulsory part of the curriculum and most classroom cupboards contained illustrations of Biblical scenes that could be unrolled at the appropriate times throughout the year to illustrate the teaching of Bible stories.

Teaching methods were thorough, if unimaginative. The pupils sat in orderly rows at standardised desks and chairs while the teacher addressed them from the blackboard. Each day in the classroom began with the reading out of the register, and any child late or absent without a good reason was likely to be punished; truancy officers patrolled the streets on the lookout for children of school age during school hours. Children absent from school were as likely as not working. One English country headmistress complained in 1890:

'Field-work, gathering stones, cow-keeping and farmwork has reduced the average. 35 out of 61 attended. It is impossible, in my opinion, to teach either Geography or Grammar

OUT OF FAVOUR Unruly children could expect punishment of one kind or another.

suitable for girls, such as domestic science. There was still a built-in assumption that boys would grow up to do the work of the world and that girls were best prepared for looking after the home. There was also a strong emphasis in the schools on citizenship, on the duty owed to one's employers and to one's country, and, as such, they were training grounds for reliable workers and patriotic citizens. In addition, the organisation of elementary education on a national basis actually emphasised feelings of national identity; this was a time, according to one French historian for example, when 'peasants turned into Frenchmen'. American children throughout the nation began their day by pledging allegiance to the flag, as they had done since the end of the Civil War.

The practice of including religious instruction varied from country to country. The United States and France, for example, had a completely secular

A LITTLE LEARNING The children of the upper classes
were still often educated at home by governesses.
Inset: Cheaper than paper, the slate was used in
primary schools for written work.

the native language, perfected by means of spelling
bees, or competitions.

A standard form of handwriting was taught by
means of the careful copying of sayings in copy-
books. The children wrote on slates or with pens
dipped into the inkwells built into their desks.
Lessons and breaks for play were strictly regulated
by the ringing of bells. Punishment, if it was
required for such grave offences as talking in class,
was administered with the cane or the leather strap.

SECONDARY SCHOOLING

Elementary schooling ended for children at around
the age of 12. In Europe, with a few exceptions
such as Scotland, Switzerland, the Netherlands and
Denmark, admission to the secondary schools –
the German *Gymnasium*, the French *lycée*, the
English public school and grammar school – was
largely limited to the sons of the wealthy or
professional classes; for example, in Germany only
8 per cent of youth attended the *Gymnasium* or any

owing to the bad attendances caused by the farmers
sending the children out on the fields.'

Much was learned by rote; the arithmetical
tables, in particular, had to be got off by heart and
spelling, especially in schools where English was

EYEWITNESS

AN ENGLISH COUNTRY SCHOOL

Florence Spurling became headmistress of the local village school
at Akenfield in Suffolk, England,
in 1900. She kept a diary of the
day-to-day activities of the school,
from which these extracts are
taken. They illustrate the way in
which patriotism and discipline
played a central role in the
education of children.

❝ 1900 Taught the whole school
a new song – 'The old folks at
home'. The average attendance is
43.2. Commenced the Royal Copy
Books. Gave special attention to
arithmetic.

(March) Owing to the very cold
East winds a large amount of
sickness prevails.

Peter and Nellie Whittle were
kept at home two days this week to
go stone-picking with their mother.
1901 Alice Tilney, being 13, left
school on Monday to go into
service. Charles Deering was
caned (four stripes) for repeated
disobedience and the Brown
brothers were caned (one stripe
each) for stealing apples. All the
big boys were caned on Wednes-
day for throwing stones at men
working in the opposite field. John
Marriage was expelled (November) for refusing to obey me. But
he apologised the next morning,
so I allowed him to come to
school again. I administered corporal punishment to William Brown

(December) for insubordination.
1902 Eight children are still away
with the water-pox. Average attendance, 72 per cent. Government
Report: 'Sound foundations are
being laid here.'
1907 Empire Day (30th May) was
celebrated in School today. Her
Ladyship kindly lent 20 flags and
the children were taught to salute
the Union Jack. Lessons were
given on the Union Jack and the
'Growth and Extent of the British
Empire'. Several patriotic songs
were sung, and the afternoon was
spent in organised games. Three
selected compositions on 'Empire
Day' were dispatched to one of the
colonies. ❞

schools. Only after 1900 did science and modern languages begin to acquire equal status with the classics for university admission. The USA led in this respect; in Britain, France and Germany, although science and modern subjects were taught, the idea persisted until 1914 and beyond that a classical education was the only fitting one for the upper and professional classes. Germany, for example, had three main types of secondary school: the classical *Gymnasium*, the *Realgymnasium* (which required Latin but not Greek) and the *Oberrealschule*, which specialised in modern languages and science. However, until the early 1900s only graduates of the *Gymnasium* were admitted to study for the professions, including law and medicine. The Kaiser himself criticised this system: 'It is our duty,' he protested, 'to educate young men to become young Germans, and not young Greeks and Romans.'

other kind of secondary school, and France, where the system was rigorously selective, had the lowest percentage of pupils in secondary schools of any Western country – even as late as 1909, fewer than 150 000 French children were enrolled in secondary schools. And in the USA, by 1910 more than 90 per cent of children were receiving only six years of elementary education. In England, by 1910 there were 1200 secondary schools supported by local taxes and national subsidies, but these nonetheless charged fees and were therefore beyond the means of most working-class people.

The study of Latin and Greek still dominated the curriculum of the secondary

EDUCATION FOR ALL
Afro-American children take part in a school music lesson in 1910.

ADOLF HITLER AT SCHOOL

ADOLF HITLER, born in Braunau, Austria, in 1889, received good reports from the various grammar schools he attended as a boy. He was noted as a bright student, with a tendency to laziness and a strong interest in history and art. In 1905 his parents sent him to the *Realschule* in Linz. The *Realschule* specialised in modern subjects, as distinct from the *Gymnasium*, which specialised in the classics, and the fact that this type of school was chosen for him suggests that, unlike his father, he was not intended for a civil service career.

At the *Realschule* he was a failure, twice having to repeat a grade. His report cards referred to him as 'unsatisfactory' in diligence; he received reasonably good marks only in 'conduct', drawing and mathematics; in all other subjects he rarely received marks better than 'adequate'. His 1905 report declared him 'unsatisfactory' in German, mathematics and stenography, and failed him in geography and history, which he himself called his favourite subjects. He later claimed that he had no friends at the school. A contemporary who shared a boarding-house with him for a time recalled: 'None of the five other boys made friends with him. Whereas we schoolmates naturally called one another *du*, he addressed us as *Sie*, and we also said *Sie* to him and did not even think there was anything odd about it.'

It is likely that as an unsophisticated country boy, the son of a minor civil servant, Hitler felt out of place among the other boys, who were mainly the children of academics, successful businessmen and the upper classes. Whatever the reason for his failure, in 1905 he left school with what he was to call 'an elemental hatred' and soon after went to Vienna to seek fame and fortune as an artist.

TRADITIONAL TEXTS
A Spanish school book of 1904 explains the geometry of Euclid.

Teaching of the classics was largely a matter of rote-learning of grammar and the translation of standard passages of prose and verse. Most young men emerged from six or more years of Latin with little more than a smattering of the language. But for the academically gifted, the classics were still living languages. It was noted, for example, that in the years of their friendship in the early 1900s, the Austrian Sigmund Freud and the Swiss Carl Gustav Jung frequently switched into Latin or Greek during their conversations. Medical students were required to prove knowledge of Latin before they could qualify as doctors, and serious newspapers frequently used Latin phrases, confident that their readership were familiar with them.

England, then as now, was unique in the extent to which its upper and middle classes sent their sons away to boarding school, whether to such ancient ones as Eton and Winchester or to one of the scores of public schools that had been founded during the 19th century and that provided the models for similar schools in Australia, New Zealand, Canada and even in India and South Africa, and to some extent for the more exclusive preparatory or private secondary schools in the United States.

The public schools emphasised the classics, but they departed from their continental European counterparts in the importance they placed on team sports and on 'manliness' in general. Conditions were deliberately made spartan. Food was plain, if not actually bad. Cold baths were a recommended part of the regime, and many boys came away with memories of breaking the ice on the morning washing bowl. Punishment, whether administered by masters or senior boys, could be severe; the flogging block was still in use at many schools.

In most of the public schools there was a strong divide between a minority of 'aesthetes', who professed a liking for study and the arts, and a

SEATS OF LEARNING   There is an almost relaxed
atmosphere in this French classroom of the early 1900s.
Inset: Boys at the English boarding school Christ's
Hospital relax or study in their dormitory.

majority of 'hearties' who positively boasted of
their philistinism. The more exclusive and expensive of these schools were providing a leisured
class with valuable social contacts and at least a
veneer of cultivation; the majority, meanwhile,
were preparing young men either for the professions or for service in one part or another of the
Empire. At best, the public schools prepared
young men to live uncomplainingly in places where
conditions might be rough, and inculcated a sense
of duty and 'fair play' – many of them,
for example, gave up time and money to running
clubs for poor boys in inner-city areas – but there
were also strong undercurrents of bullying and of
homosexuality.

UNIVERSITY LIFE

If only a minority of the population received secondary education in the 1900s, those who went on
to university were a small elite of the wealthy and
the especially gifted. The English philosopher

DIVISION OF LABOUR   Girls are taught how to
wash clothes at a London housewifery centre.

97

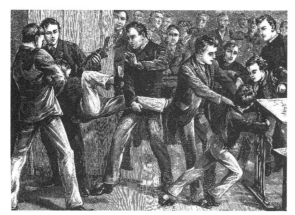

BULLY BOYS   **Bullying was a feature of the English public schools.**

Bertrand Russell, who was aristocratic, wealthy and supremely gifted, became an undergraduate at Cambridge University in 1890. Later in life, he reflected that he could not entirely condemn the system, even though it was so privileged, because, in his experience, it had produced such excellence; among his contemporaries as undergraduates, all of them wealthy and well connected, were some of the most brilliant men of the day. Typical of them was Charles Percy Sanger, one of his first friends at the university:

'We used to work on mathematics together. He was incredibly quick, and would be halfway through solving a problem before I had understood the question....He was also a very good economist, and he could read an incredible number of languages, including such out-of-the-way items as Magyar and Finnish. I used to go on walking tours with him in Italy, and he always made me do all the conversation with innkeepers, but when I was reading Italian, I found that his knowledge of the language was vastly greater than mine.'

Yet Russell held the teaching at the university in general in very low esteem. He and the men of

---

EYEWITNESS

AN ENGLISH PUBLIC SCHOOL

The English poet and novelist Robert Graves was sent to Charterhouse, one of the most famous of the English public schools, in the years immediately before the First World War, where he came up against a rigid caste system.

❛   The school consisted of about six hundred boys, whose chief interests were games and romantic friendships. Everyone despised school work; the scholars were not concentrated in a single dormitory house as at Winchester or Eton, but divided among ten, and known as "pro's". Unless good at games, and able to pretend that they hated work even more than the non-scholars, and ready whenever called on to help these with their work, they always had a bad time. I happened to be a scholar who really liked work, and the apathy of the classrooms surprised and disappointed me. My first term, I was left alone more or less, it being a rule that new boys should be neither encouraged nor baited. The other boys seldom addressed me except to send me on errands, or coldly point out breaches of school convention....

The "bloods" were the ruling caste of Charterhouse; the eleventh man in the football eleven, though he might be a member of the lower-fourth form, enjoyed far more prestige than the most brilliant scholar in the sixth. Even 'Head of School' was an empty title....

The social code of Charterhouse rested on a strict caste system; the caste marks, or *post-te's*, being slight distinctions in dress. A new boy had no privileges at all; a boy in his second term might wear a knitted tie instead of a plain one; a boy in his second year might wear coloured socks; the third year gave most of the main privileges – turned-down collars, coloured handkerchiefs, a coat with a long roll, and so on; fourth year, a few more, such as the right to get up raffles; but peculiar distinctions were reserved for the bloods. These included light-grey flannel trousers, butterfly collars, jackets slit up the back, and the right of walking arm-in-arm. ❜

BEST OF THE BEST Students attend a physics lecture at the Ecole Polytechnique, Paris, one of the French *grandes écoles* designed to educate an elite. Right: Bertrand Russell (seated on the ground, centre) surrounded by some of his contemporaries at Cambridge.

genius that he met there acquired a wide and deep education through their own private study, from each other, and from a handful of inspiring teachers.

Russell and his brilliant friends were a minority at the Oxford and Cambridge colleges of the time. For the majority, academic work imposed a light burden. The university years were a blissful interval between the rigours of public school and whatever career one was to enter or responsibilities one was to take up afterwards.

The wealthy undergraduate had a set of rooms of his own and a manservant to wait on him. The college kitchen would supply food and wine for luncheon or dinner parties in his rooms and there were clubs and societies to suit every taste. In the summer there was plenty of time for cricket or for boating parties on the river. In winter there was hunting.

Richard Verney, who later became Lord Willoughby de Broke, left New College, Oxford, with 'an easy degree, cricket, hunting and driving four horses; the last three being very necessary accomplishments to the

ACADEMIC HONOURS German women students march proudly at a university ceremony. Behind them, male students wear the uniform of their duelling societies.

life that seemed to be indicated to me', that is, the life of a country landowner with a passionate love of foxhunting. Verney was probably a more representative Oxbridge undergraduate than Bertrand Russell.

THE GERMAN TRADITION

All the countries of Europe and North America had their great universities, some of which were very ancient, but the supremacy of German university education was recognised worldwide. Altogether there were 21 German universities and higher

A WRITER AT PRINCETON

SCOTT FITZGERALD went to Princeton University, in New Jersey, in 1913. He fell in love with the place, writing romantically of the campus where 'topping all, climbing with clear blue aspiration, (were) the great dreaming spires of Holder and Cleveland towers'. In one of his novels, *This Side of Paradise*, he was to describe the upperclassmen as they marched arm-in-arm through University Place singing a college song, led by the football captain, 'slim and defiant, as if aware that this year the hopes of the college rested on him, that his hundred-and-sixty pounds were expected to dodge to victory through the heavy blue and crimson lines'. Varsity football players were worshipped; scholars were not.

As a freshman, Fitzgerald was bound by strict rules. He was expected to be in his room by 9 pm, was forbidden to smoke a pipe on campus, and was obliged to wear a black skullcap, known as a 'dink' or 'beanie'. He learned the social distinctions of the place, which marked out the natural leaders

YOUNG WRITER For Fitzgerald, success began in his student days.

from the 'scuts' or 'birds', as the lesser men were called. He boarded at a house known as 'The Morgue', ate in the Commons with the other freshmen, and cut classes while he wrote and waited his chance to join the Triangle, a club that put on musical comedies.

In 1914, as Europe went to war, Fitzgerald triumphed when a script of his was finally accepted for performance by the Triangle. The following year, Fitzgerald's

second, groups of undergraduates began visiting the sophomores to interview them for membership of Princeton's exclusive clubs: he would have liked to join Ivy, which he described as 'detached and breathlessly aristocratic', but he received offers from Cottage, Cap and Gown, Quadrangle and Cannon, and finally settled for Cottage, one of the biggest clubs.

He was soon writing for *The Tiger*, a humorous magazine, and the *Nassau Lit*, Princeton's literary magazine, drinking pitchers of beer at 'the Nass', the tavern where members of all the clubs gathered, and wooing his first serious girlfriend. Newspaper critics and Broadway producers were taking an interest in his work. What with all these activities, his academic studies suffered badly, and he narrowly missed having to repeat his junior year.

In April 1917, the United States declared war on Germany, and at the end of that year Fitzgerald left Princeton, commissioned as a second lieutenant and bound for training at Fort Leavenworth.

technical schools, with a total enrolment of over 60 000 students. Foreign students attended German universities, especially Berlin, Leipzig, Munich, Heidelberg, Gottingen and Freiburg, in large numbers. The number of American students

THE BEST DAYS OF YOUR LIFE An undergraduate's room at Yale in 1908. Inset: A group of students attending a Midwest university in 1912 setting off on a field trip. The university took both male and female undergraduates.

at German universities steadily declined during the 1900s, however, as the reputation of American universities improved, but the German influence on American tertiary education was powerful: the graduate school, the PhD degree, the seminar, the research laboratory and the scientific journal were all ideas imported from Germany.

Already exclusive in that they accepted only a very small and privileged percentage of the population, the older universities in most countries also cultivated their own exclusiveness within the

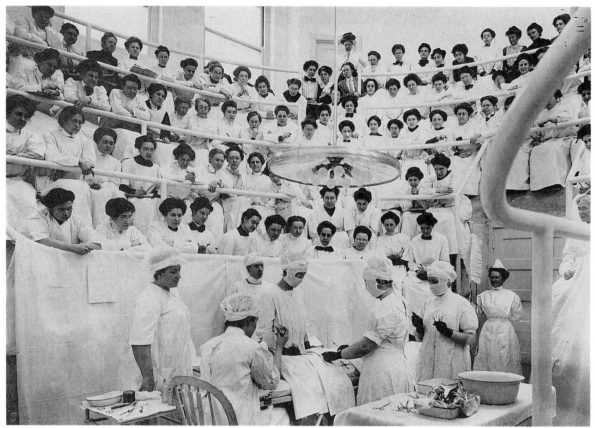

ANATOMY FOR WOMEN **By the 1890s, women were being admitted as medical students in Western countries.**

student body as a whole. The Ivy League colleges of democratic America, for example, had their clubs, or fraternities, with their subtle but crucially important distinctions in social prestige, their rituals and their – sometimes cruel – initiation

A MATTER OF HONOUR **German students take part in a duel, the** *Mensur,* **in which facial scars were often inflicted.**

ceremonies, during which, on some rare occasions, young men died from heart attacks caused by sheer terror.

Aside from academic excellence, German universities, too, had their own distinctive social character, harking back to the Middle Ages when many of them were founded. Most, for example, had their *Verbindungen* or 'fighting corps', student societies with esoteric rules and rituals, distinctive uniforms and enormous prestige. They were given to beer-drinking bouts, drinking-songs and fighting with the townspeople, but the most distinctive of their activities was the *Mensur* or student duel. This was fought with the *Schlaeger* or heavy rapier and part of the face was left unprotected so that participants could obtain the duelling scars that were regarded as marks of honour. There might have been social reformers, or even revolutionaries, among German students in the early years of the century, but the general character of the universities at the time was deeply conservative and nationalistic.

HEALTH AND MEDICINE

Overcrowding and bad diet still bred disease and high infant mortality, but improvements

in public health provisions, together with greater understanding of the causes of diseases

and how they spread, were leading to an increase in life expectancy.

SLUM CLEARANCE   Urban slums persisted, but efforts were made to clear them, as here in Kennington, London.

THE END OF the 19th century and beginning of the 20th was a watershed in the history of disease. Society was taking its 'modern' shape, with huge numbers of people crowded together in cities as never before, but modern antibiotics and medicines were not yet available to treat the effects of that urban crowding in terms of disease.

City life, especially for the poor, still went hand in hand with epidemic and infectious disease and with chronic sickness related to damp, stress, foul air, contaminated food and malnutrition. Research carried out in Britain in 1905-9, for example, suggested that nearly half of all working-class women were in chronic poor health, and, although the British working-class diet was particularly bad, there is no reason to suppose that conditions were much better in the major cities of Europe and North America. In the 1890s, infant mortality in New York's slum districts was running at 1500

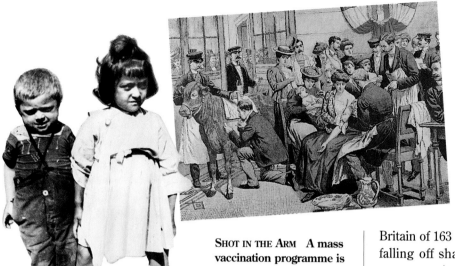

SHOT IN THE ARM A mass vaccination programme is carried out in France in 1905. Left: Improvements in diet helped to combat diseases such as rickets.

deaths a week during the summer months.

Despite these factors, the overall death rate was declining. In Britain, for example, life expectancy for middle-aged women showed a marked improvement in the 1880s and for middle-aged men in the 1890s. But infant mortality remained high, reaching a peak in Britain of 163 deaths per 1000 births in 1899 before falling off sharply after 1902. But there were, of course, regional and social variations: in general, mortality was higher in large towns and among the poor, lower in the country, in the more salubrious suburbs and among the comfortably off. If there

A WOMAN DOCTOR IN THE SLUMS OF BOSTON

S. Josephine Baker graduated as a doctor in New York in 1898, and subsequently began work in Boston. The conditions of poverty and violence that she found there deeply shocked her. One day, she was called to see a woman who was expecting a baby.

❛ I thought I already knew something about how filthy a tenement room could be. But this was something special, particularly in the amount of insect life. One dingy oil lamp, by the light of which I could barely make out the woman in labour, lying on a heap of straw in one corner. Four stunted children, too frightened to make any noise, huddled together in a far corner. The floor was littered with scraps of food, too old to be easily identifiable, but all contributors to the odour of the

place. Cockroaches and bedbugs crawled about everywhere. The only place to wash up in was, as usual, an old tin basin, rusted and ragged at the edge. All of it was the nth power of abject, discouraged squalor. But the ugliest detail was a man, also lying on the floor because he was apparently too drunk to get up. But he was all too capable of speech.

The moment I approached my patient I discovered that her back was one raw, festering sore. She said that her husband had thrown a kettle of scalding water over her a few days before. That accusation brought him to his feet crazy with rage, threatening me and her, toppling and lurching all over the place.

I knew that could not go on. I had to get him out of the way. As he wavered toward me, waving

his clenched fist and uttering verbal filth, I ran out into the hall. He followed me as I intended. I had thought of running in quickly again and seeing if the door would lock. But then, as he lurched after me, he crossed the stair-head and, with instinctive reaction, I doubled my fist and hit him. I weighed hardly half as much as he, but he was practically incapable of standing up, and this frantic tap of mine was strategically placed. He toppled backward, struck about a third of the way down the rather long stair and slid to the bottom with a hideous crash. Then there was absolute silence. I had taken my opportunity and the result was evident. I went back into the room, pushed a piece of furniture against the closed door and delivered the baby undisturbed. ❜

PLAGUE Syphilis was a scourge throughout Europe until Paul Ehrlich discovered a vaccine for it.

was an overall improvement in public health, it was due at least as much to civil engineering works (notably improved public sewage systems) and to public administration (slum clearance, the inspection of food markets and so forth) as to advances in medical knowledge and skills.

During the 1870s and 80s, great advances were made in the control of infection and disease. These were largely a result of the work of the French chemist and microbiologist Louis Pasteur on the germ theory of disease, the English surgeon Joseph Lister on antisepsis surgery – procedures aimed at preventing the spread of infection – and the German bacteriologist Robert Koch on the identification of microbes. Thanks to their work, people were aware by the 1890s that disease was spread by micro-organisms and that many could be checked by aseptic surgery (surgery carried out by 'sterilised' surgeons using sterilised instruments and materials), by improvements in sanitation or by vaccination.

In Edwardian times, there was an obsessive concern with cleanliness, amounting almost to

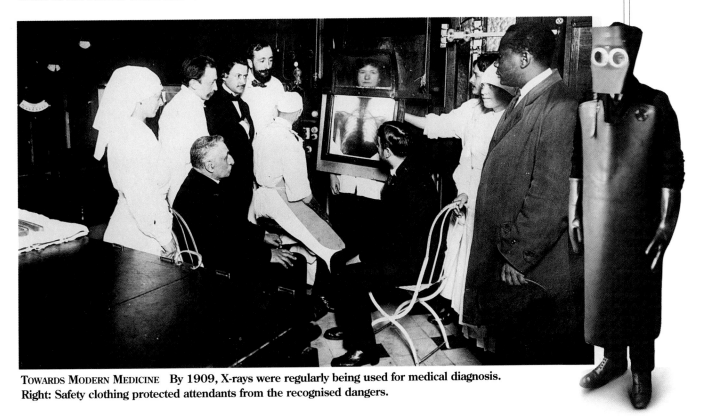

TOWARDS MODERN MEDICINE By 1909, X-rays were regularly being used for medical diagnosis.
Right: Safety clothing protected attendants from the recognised dangers.

A VICTIM OF HER OWN SUCCESS

DISCOVERER OF RADIOACTIVITY Marie Curie died of leukaemia, almost certainly as a result of her own researches into radioactivity.

MARIE CURIE was born Manya Sklodowska in Warsaw in 1867. Strikingly gifted from childhood, she received a sound education at the Russian lycée – the Russians at that time being more advanced than many other nations in offering higher education to women.

After working for a time as a governess and teacher, in 1891 she went to Paris, where she studied at the Sorbonne, living in a garret on a diet of bread, butter and tea. In 1893 she graduated with honours. In 1894, now called Marie, she met a fellow scientist, Pierre Curie, whom she married the following year.

Working together on physics and chemistry and in particular on the question of the radiation emitted by such materials as uranium, the Curies established the existence of three different types of particle caused by radioactivity, a term first employed by Marie Curie in 1898.

In that year the two also announced the discovery of two entirely new elements, polonium (called after Marie's native Poland) and radium. In 1900, Pierre was appointed lecturer in physics at the Sorbonne and Marie became a lecturer in physics at a school for girls. In 1903, they were awarded the Nobel prize for physics for their discovery of radioactivity.

Pierre, appointed professor of physics at the Sorbonne in 1904, was tragically killed in a street accident in 1906. Marie, though devastated, dedicated herself to completing their work. A month after Pierre's death, she was apppointed to the chair he had vacated, becoming the first woman ever to teach at the Sorbonne. In 1911 she was awarded the Nobel prize for chemistry for her discovery of radium and polonium and for her isolation of pure radium.

Throughout the First World War she was to work on the application of X-rays to medical diagnosis, especially for the treatment of wounded soldiers. She died in 1934, of leukaemia caused by exposure to radiation. Her daughter Irene went on to form a scientific partnership with her husband, Frederick Joliot-Curie, remarkably similar to that of Marie and Pierre.

FIT FOR LIFE In Britain, in particular, there was anxiety in the early 1900s about the national level of physical fitness, and exercise routines were encouraged for both men and women.

panic; middle-class people developed a horror of dust and dirt in their own homes and, aware of the limited facilities for personal hygiene available to the urban and rural working class, tended to shrink from them as carriers of disease. In the elementary schools, great efforts were made to inculcate habits of personal cleanliness among the poor as a matter of public interest.

CONTROLLING DISEASES

Bacteria and viruses and their relationship with disease had been identified. New forms of drug treatment and painkillers had been developed. Techniques of inoculation, vaccination, sterilisation and anaesthesia had improved. American Army surgeons, after research in Cuba in the early 1900s, had established the connection of the mosquito with yellow fever. After similar research carried out in India showed the mosquito's connection with malaria, mosquito control through swamp drainage and crop-spraying, together with the use

of quinine as a treatment for the disease, greatly reduced its incidence.

In Europe and other temperate parts of the world, deaths from such diseases as diphtheria, scarlet fever, smallpox and typhoid fever became relatively rare; tuberculosis remained a serious problem, though it was beginning to be controlled through isolation and fresh-air treatment in sanatoria. Deaths from smallpox had been practically eliminated in Northern and Western Europe by 1900; deaths from scarlet fever had been greatly reduced, and mortality from tuberculosis was about half that of the mid-Victorian period. Influenza, pneumonia and syphilis, however, were still major killers throughout the Western world. Venereal disease was a major problem throughout the whole of Europe;

WELFARE STATE Workers could get health-care insurance.

107

MILITARY NURSES   French Red Cross nurses served in Morocco in 1908. Many more would be needed after 1914.

reports suggested that it was endemic throughout all classes of the urban population, including the very young.

In general, by 1900 the very rich and the very poor were benefiting from medical care infinitely better than would have been available in the 1850s. For the classes in between, medicine was often an unaffordable luxury. Access to skilled specialist treatment often depended on the accident of living near one of the great teaching hospitals, whose location, of course, might bear no relation to modern population distribution. By the end of the prewar period, anxiety about the spread of infection and about the growth of a physically 'degenerate' underclass was leading to the view that even the private health of individuals was a matter of public concern. This led to school medical examinations in many European countries, to the first proposals for a state medical service and to legislation such as Britain's 1911 National Insurance Act, which provided sickness insurance and basic health care for the whole of the employed working population.

START THE DAY WITH CEREAL

North Americans led the way in the development of breakfast cereals. The first was Shredded Wheat, produced in 1893 by Henry Perky. He began production on a national scale in 1895. In that year Dr John Kellogg announced his Granose Flakes, also made from wheat. His brother William introduced corn flakes in 1898. The first breakfast cereal to reach Britain was Force wheat flakes, from Canada. Breakfast cereals remained unknown in continental Europe before the First World War.

HOSPITAL CARE

By the early 1900s the idea of modern hospital care was beginning to establish itself. Hospitals were becoming regarded as agencies for the care and prevention of disease rather than, as they had been earlier in the 19th century, refuges for the destitute and the dying. However, new hospitals with bright, airy wards were still relatively rare in Europe as a

INFANT CARE Many more children were being cared for in hospital, as here in London's Vincent Square.

whole; many were still grim institutions that people were afraid to enter. In some, for example, patients suffering from infectious diseases were lowered into virtual pits; food and water were let down to them in baskets, but they were otherwise left to recover or die.

In most major cities there were voluntary hospitals maintained by fees, subscriptions and endowments. Although only the very poor were entitled to free health care, in practice many of these hospitals were offering free in and out-patient care to their local population, and by 1900 millions of workers were covered by some kind of contributory sickness insurance, sometimes through their own trade unions. Nurses were by now trained and respected medical personnel rather than the bed-makers and chamber-pot carriers of earlier times, and the nursing profession was becoming something remarkable – possibly unique – for its time in the way it was bringing together young women from all classes of society. Again, patient care in the form of hygiene, isolation, rest and decent nutrition contrib-uted at least as much as the admin-istration of drugs to recovery from

CARRYING THE SICK
The motorised ambulance was an early development of the motor car. This one dates from 1906. Above right: The doctor's role and status was greatly enhanced; they came to be seen as pillars of society.

disease. But it remained the case that the vast majority of people received medical treatment – and were born and died – in their own homes. Doctors as a matter of course visited sick patients in their homes, and were among the first people to use the motor car as a professional aid rather than as a leisure vehicle; although the country doctor in his pony and trap was still a familiar sight until the outbreak of the First World War.

Doctors had grown greatly in status as medical science developed. In the mid-19th century, the doctor had been a rather suspect character; by 1914 both general practitioners and specialists were enjoying high social prestige, and upper and middle-class households had grown used to enjoying a fee-paying relationship with a 'family doctor'. This new prestige was resented by the professional rivals the qualified doctors had downgraded or displaced: the midwives, the pharmacists and the homeopaths.

One of the most important advances of the 1890s was in paediatrics and child care. Earlier in the century, child-birth had been left to the course of nature and the assistance, at the time of birth, of a midwife. By the 1890s, increased under-standing of obstetrics and

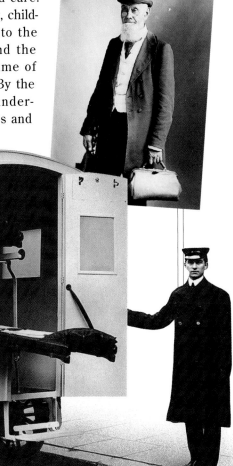

gynaecology, and of the importance of hygienic conditions, had greatly reduced the numbers of women dying in childbirth. By the 1900s, pregnant women were receiving prenatal instruction to reduce birth defects and problem deliveries.

Despite advances in orthodox medicine, a belief in 'folk' medicine persisted, especially in rural areas. Some of this 'folk' medicine – for example the rural New Englander's deep faith in the virtues of honey and cider-vinegar – is being looked upon with favour again by doctors today. In both town and country there was a large, and quite unrestricted, market for quack remedies and patent medicines of all kinds – a major source of advertising revenue in newspapers – as well as for practitioners of what would now be called 'fringe' medicine, such as herbalists and homeopaths. Jesse Boot, who founded Britain's largest chain of retail chemist shops, was

himself the son of an itinerant herbalist and healer, and many such people could still be found travelling around the country districts of Europe and North America. The selling of quack medicines probably reached its most outlandish form in the American West, where it was combined with travelling shows such as the Kickapoo Indian Medicine Company, which laid on a spectacular entertainment before inviting the audience to buy 'World Famous Kickapoo Indian Sagwa', described in advertisements as a 'panacea for all ailments'.

A FIRST IN DENTISTRY

The first professional, qualified woman dentist was an American, Miss Lucy Hobbs, who graduated in 1866. The first woman to qualify in Britain, in 1892, was Miss Lilian Murray. When, as a schoolgirl, she declared her intention to train for the profession, her headmistress declared: 'How absurd, child! There is no such thing as a woman dentist.'

ROUGH AND READY   For dentistry, country people often still had to resort to practitioners at country fairs.
Inset: Itinerant sellers of patent medicines relied on showmanship.

RELIGION OLD AND NEW

Religious doubt spread and church attendance declined, but the religious impulse remained strong.

Some people turned to other forms of spiritualism, and even to the occult, while others pursued

their political and social beliefs with religious fervour.

GOOD AS GOLD   Middle-class children are dressed in their best clothes to attend church.

ONE OF THE most striking features of the last years of the 19th century was a marked decline in religious belief and in church attendance, at least as far as orthodox religion was concerned, especially among the educated classes at one end of society and the urban working class at the other. For intellectuals, the scientific advances and the new Biblical criticism of the 19th century had shed doubt on the truth of scripture and weakened the authority of the Church. Charles Darwin's theory of evolution, now generally accepted by the educated classes, and geological evidence for the antiquity of the world, made the account of Creation given in Genesis unacceptable in its literal sense to many of them, while comparative study of the scriptures had shown up inconsistencies that called into question even the fundamental narrative of the Gospels.

The working men, and to a lesser extent, the women, who had moved from the country to the new industrial towns of Europe and North America tended to leave their former religion behind them, and turned to the secular state for those things, such as poor relief and education, that had previously been provided mainly by the Church. In France in 1905, in an urban population of nearly 8 million, there were only an estimated 600 000 practising believers; in that year the French government withdrew all state recognition and financial support from all religious groups, bringing the Church in France into a state of crisis.

The decline in religious belief was much more marked among Protestants than among Roman Catholics, for whose womenfolk at least the neighbourhood church was still an important focus of everyday life. The Protestant churches, and to

UNBENDING FAITH A French Carmelite nun, a member of a strict Catholic order, reads aloud to her Sisters from a devotional work. Above: Religious faith remained strong in Catholic countries and in rural areas.

some extent the Roman Catholic Church before 1903, attempted to adjust belief in the light of modern scientific views and to involve religion in social and economic reform. However, this kind of 'modernism', as it was called, was totally rejected by the Roman Catholic Church during the pontificate of Pius X (1903-14), who abhorred everything modern in culture, learning and thought. Pius called modernism 'not a heresy, but the summation and essence of every heresy', put several modernist books on the Index of Forbidden Books, and demanded that all teachers in seminaries and clerics before ordination take an oath denouncing modernism. Despite this profound conservatism of belief, the Roman Catholic Church succeeded in holding the allegiance of the urban working class to a far greater extent than did the Protestant churches.

MANNERS IN CHURCH

For the middle classes, attending church was a social as well as a religious activity, and good manners were expected. Madge of the English magazine *Truth* advises:

❝ Lounging is a habit of the day, and there are men who get themselves into marvellously corkscrew attitudes, in church as elsewhere. Fidgety men are more so in church than anywhere else. Sometimes they even produce a cough wherewith to amuse themselves, though they are not troubled with it at any other time. The charm of a reposeful manner is denied to them. Reverence for the sacred place conduces to a quiet manner; but this is not always felt by those who attend public worship. The conventional idea seems to be that such assemblies are merely phases of social life; that it is respectable to be seen there; and that the service and the sermon are things to be worried through in deference to a prevalent idea that they form part of an institution that is generally regarded as excellent. The small minority are those who regard church services in their true light as lifting the thoughts above earthly things, and yet by no means unfitting them for earth. ❞

SOCIAL EVENT A Church of England congregation around 1912 is smartly dressed and on its best behaviour.

Church attendance became a rural and middle-class custom. Few people felt compelled by the authority of the clergy to attend church every Sunday, as they had earlier in the 19th century, but did so from a sense that it was the proper thing to do. Sunday church was to a considerable extent a social occasion. Many of the hymns sung were cheerful, and sermons were generrally shorter than in more earnest times.

Clergymen in the established churches, drawn almost entirely from the middle and upper classes, sometimes even from the aristocracy, rarely risked either scolding their congregations with moral or religious fervour, or boring them with lengthy scriptural disquisitions.

Socially and politically conservative, and associated with the State and with the Establishment, the established Protestant churches simply had no appeal to the working classes, who gave their allegiance to the trade union, the friendly society or the local café or pub. (This was less true of the dissenting churches and in Scotland, where the more democratic traditions of the Kirk gave it a continuing appeal at least to

THE WORD **A German preacher expounds from the baroque pulpit of an earlier age.**

sections of the 'respectable' working class.) Yet, except perhaps in France, where an atheist tradition had been established at the time of the Revolution, consciously declared atheism was rare among working men; they might not have their children baptised, or marry in church, but it was rare to have a funeral without some kind of religious rite.

KEEPING SUNDAY SPECIAL

For those who continued to practise the Christian religion, great emphasis was placed on the sanctity of the Sabbath Day. In Catholic countries, Sunday afternoons tended to be regarded as a time of leisure; in Protestant countries the whole day was emphatically a Day of Rest. Churchgoing called for the putting on of one's best clothes – a fashionable church was often the place where a new hat or dress made its first appearance – and these were then kept on for the rest of the day.

Few homes still required, as they had earlier in the 19th century, that only devotional books might be read on a Sunday, but card-playing and other frivolous amusements were frowned upon, places of public amusement were closed and children were forbidden to play noisy games. Sunday, for the respectable middle classes, was a day for quiet family walks and the visiting of relatives, and perhaps for the singing of hymns around the family piano. There were many

GOD'S SOLDIER
A young woman wears the earliest uniform of members of the Salvation Army.

MAGICIAN

In the late 19th century there was a revival of interest in magic and the occult. Typical of this was the foundation in 1898 of the Order of the Golden Dawn, whose members included Aleister Crowley. Crowley was an excellent chess-player, explorer and mountaineer, and a poet, but his keenest interest was in magic, with a strong sexual element. This was to lead to his vilification in the popular press and the title of 'the wickedest man in the world'. He spent much of his life in exile abroad.

SCIENCE AND HEALTH

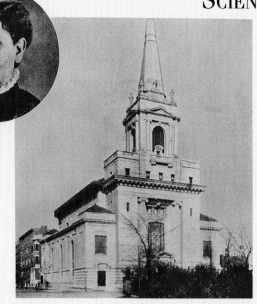

SPIRITUAL HEALING The first Christian Science church to be built in New York City was one of several branches of the movement established by Mary Baker Eddy.

MARY BAKER EDDY had founded Christian Science in the 1870s after her own recovery from what she had believed to be a fatal accident. She attributed this recovery to her readings of the New Testament. After years of study, she came to believe that she had discovered the means by which Jesus had healed the sick and raised the dead, and began to teach metaphysical, or spiritual, healing. Central to her thought was her insistence that healing was never brought about by drugs or medicines, which she and her followers rejected in favour of prayer and affirmative thinking.

In 1875 she set out her beliefs in the first edition of *Science and Health*. Together with the Bible, this was to be regarded as the scripture of the new faith. In 1879 she and her students founded the First Church of Christ, Scientist, in Boston, and in 1881 she opened the Massachusetts Metaphysical College.

During the course of the 1880s, the new doctrine spread across the USA, but teachers began to show a tendency to add their own personal interpretations of the faith. In 1889 Mrs Eddy began to assert complete control, claiming that only her own teachings represented the truth of the movement. She insisted that all local Christian Science churches were branches of the Mother Church in Boston and replaced pastors by readers; henceforth all sermons were to consist of readings from the Bible and from *Science and Health*. She also published a set of instructions, the *Manual of the Mother Church*, which, among other things, demanded complete loyalty to herself and her teachings.

By 1891 *Science and Health* had reached its 56th edition and Christian Science was widespread in North America. In 1908 Mary Baker Eddy founded the *Christian Science Monitor*, still widely respected as one of the USA's leading newspapers.

Before her death in 1910 Mary Baker Eddy handed over control to a self-perpetuating board of directors, whose successors still run the movement in accordance with the *Manual*, which is regarded as inspired and perfect and which no one is allowed to amend.

who thought it wrong even to drive or travel in a train or an omnibus on the Sabbath. Especially in Protestant countries, it was a day when the din of the streets was noticeably hushed.

Although orthodox religion might be losing its appeal for many, the religious impulse, expressed in the desire for explanations of existence other than material ones, was still strong. In the last decades of the 19th century this quest for a meaning to life was channelled into a number of other courses. Atheism itself became almost a religion for some, like the British civil servant Sir Eyre Crowe, of whom it was said:

Crowe will tell you 'til you nod,
Why he does not believe in God;
But what we'd really like to know:
Does God Himself believe in Crowe?

THE RED FLAG Rosa Luxemburg was one of the founders of the German Communist Party. Inset: A Marxist revolution was defeated in Russia in 1905.

КАРИКАТУРНЫЙ
ЛИСТОКЪ ᴑᴑᴑ
ГАЗЕТЫ ГАЗЕТЪ

FOUNDERS OF THE THEOSOPHIST MOVEMENT

THEOSOPHY – the word means 'divine wisdom' – is the system of mystical philosophy associated with Madame Helena Blavatsky, who, with her companion, the American lawyer Henry Steel Olcott, founded the Theosophical Society in 1875. Of noble Russian descent, Mme Blavatsky had emigrated to the USA in 1873 after much study of the mystical tradition, especially in Hindu and Buddhist thought.

In 1878 she and Olcott moved to India, where they founded what became the international headquarters of the Theosophical Society at Adyar, near Madras. In the closing years of the 19th century other branches were founded throughout India and in the major cities of Europe.

Mme Blavatsky expounded her ideas in two principal works: *Isis Unveiled* (1877) and *The Secret Doctrine* (1888). Both she and her

LEADING LADY   Madame Blavatsky was thought by some to have mystical powers.

followers insisted that they were not founding a new religion, but unveiling a core of truth about the nature of God and of human life that lay at the heart of all the great religions. They also claimed the existence of a fraternity of Great Masters or Adepts, who have perfected themselves spiritually and now direct the

spiritual evolution of humans. The idea of spiritual evolution through reincarnation and karma – the sum of a person's existence in previous incarnations – is central to theosophical thought; the soul makes a pilgrimage towards perfection through the seven planes in which the Universe is ordered. Progress is determined by karma, cause and effect; although every human creature is free to choose his or her actions, any action taken in one's present life will have its effects in a future incarnation.

Madame Blavatsky died in 1891 and was succeeded as world leader of the movement by Olcott, although by now the American wing had largely separated itself from the rest of the Society. On Olcott's death in 1907, he was succeeded as president in India by the English woman Annie Besant, whose own writings helped greatly to strengthen the movement.

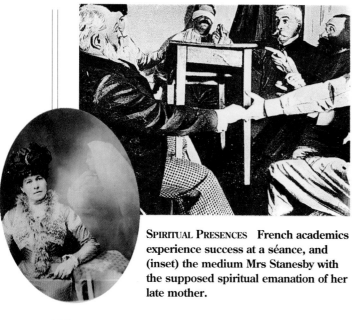

SPIRITUAL PRESENCES   French academics experience success at a séance, and (inset) the medium Mrs Stanesby with the supposed spiritual emanation of her late mother.

Others devoted themselves with near-religious fervour to movements such as Socialism and Communism, which had acquired many of the trappings and characteristics of a religion, with their prophets, their sacred books and their promise of a New Jerusalem. Still others developed an interest in Oriental religions, in Christian Science, in spiritualism – numerous spiritualist churches had been formed throughout the English-speaking world by 1900 – or in the Theosophy of Madame Blavatsky, a philosphical and religious system that incorporated aspects of Buddhism and emphasised the mystical nature of the relationship between an individual and God. A small minority of people, especially in France but elsewhere too, even turned to the practice of ritual magic and necromancy.

ENTERTAINMENT AND LEISURE

The years around 1900 witnessed the rise of the popular press, the international spread of spectator sports such as football and tennis, the continued popularity of novels and the theatre, and, above all, the dramatic emergence of the cinema as a medium of popular entertainment. The bicycle played its part in social levelling, but the upper classes stayed faithful to the traditional pursuits of hunting, shooting and fishing and the pleasures of the country-house weekend.

POPULAR ENTERTAINMENTS

During a time of innovation in the arts and entertainment that saw a revolution in the

newspaper industry, the first best-selling novels and avant-garde productions in the world of

ballet, the greatest innovation of all was the cinema.

ONE OF THE outstanding features of the end of the 19th century and the beginning of the 20th was the rise of the popular press, especially in the USA and Britain.

Mass literacy, and concentrations of population in the cities, offered a huge market for a popular daily press and popular magazines. Linotype typesetting and high-speed rotary presses made it possible to produce newspapers cheaply by the million; the amount of newsprint paper that had cost $3 in 1880 cost only $1 in 1900.

There was a revolution in the content and style of newspapers. New emphasis was put on features of interest to women, on 'muck-raking', scandal, and human interest stories – what the American newspaper publisher William Randolph Hearst called 'crime and underwear' stories. Campaigns were conducted against big business and corruption in local and national government. Sales-promoting gimmicks and stunts were introduced, and, when exciting real news was in short supply, news 'events' were created.

In Britain, newspaper proprietor Alfred Harmsworth followed the American lead with the *Daily Mail*, first published in 1896, and in 1903 he launched the *Daily Mirror*, at that time a newspaper aimed at women. The British

GET YOUR PAPER HERE! An American newspaper boy supplies the popular demand for news.

public in the 1890s were already familiar with popular magazines, such as *Tit-Bits* and Harmsworth's *Answers*, which specialised in anecdotes, riddles and scraps of information, all designed to attract the newly literate. Other new popular newspapers followed a similar formula, with a strong emphasis on sensational stories; what one of Harmsworth's associates called 'a good meaty crime' topped the list of favourites, followed by sports, wars and natural disasters.

Above all, the popular press loved headlining the 'inside story'. When Dr Crippen, the wife-murderer, was trying to escape from England to Canada with his mistress, Ethel Le Neve, on the *SS Montrose* in July 1910, the ship's captain thought he recognised him and sent a wireless message that reached Reuters and the British police. Newspaper readers on both sides of the Atlantic followed the story as the couple continued their voyage, unaware that they had been detected. They were arrested when the ship reached the St Lawrence

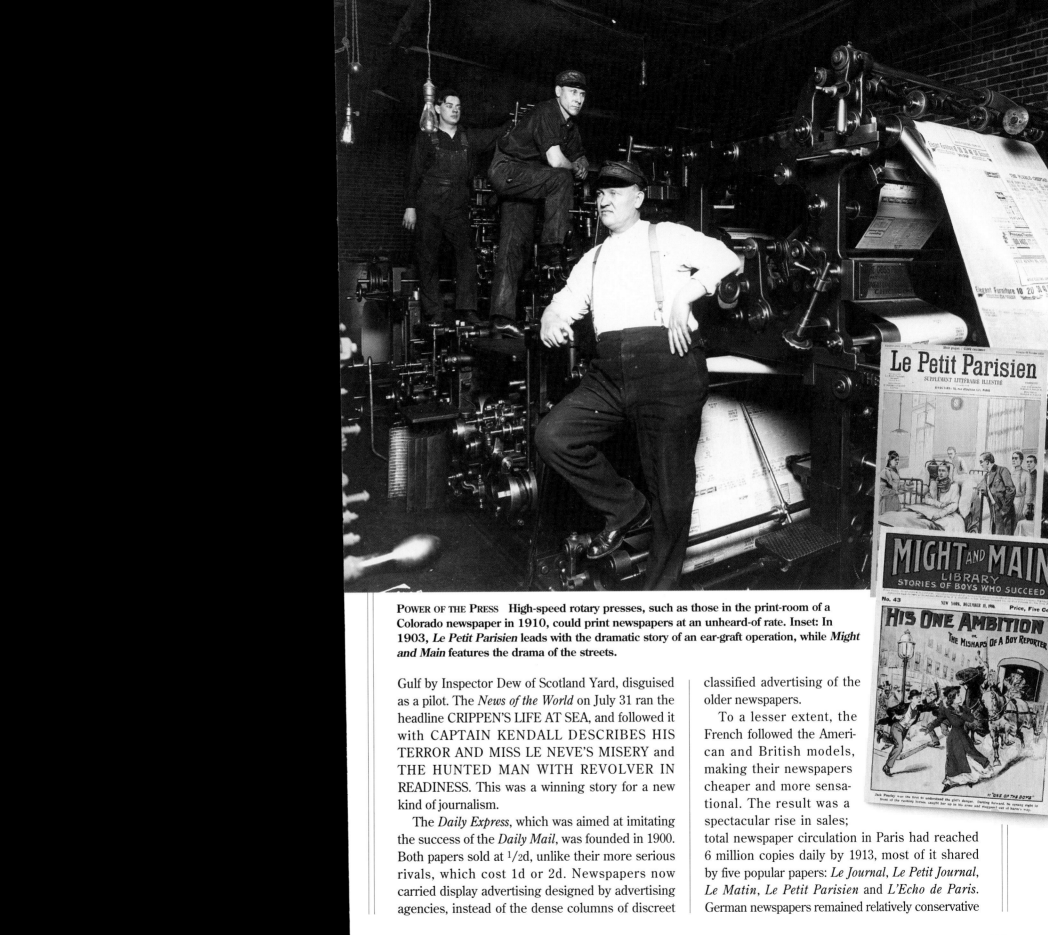

POWER OF THE PRESS   High-speed rotary presses, such as those in the print-room of a Colorado newspaper in 1910, could print newspapers at an unheard-of rate. Inset: In 1903, *Le Petit Parisien* leads with the dramatic story of an ear-graft operation, while *Might and Main* features the drama of the streets.

Gulf by Inspector Dew of Scotland Yard, disguised as a pilot. The *News of the World* on July 31 ran the headline CRIPPEN'S LIFE AT SEA, and followed it with CAPTAIN KENDALL DESCRIBES HIS TERROR AND MISS LE NEVE'S MISERY and THE HUNTED MAN WITH REVOLVER IN READINESS. This was a winning story for a new kind of journalism.

The *Daily Express*, which was aimed at imitating the success of the *Daily Mail*, was founded in 1900. Both papers sold at 1/2d, unlike their more serious rivals, which cost 1d or 2d. Newspapers now carried display advertising designed by advertising agencies, instead of the dense columns of discreet classified advertising of the older newspapers.

To a lesser extent, the French followed the American and British models, making their newspapers cheaper and more sensational. The result was a spectacular rise in sales; total newspaper circulation in Paris had reached 6 million copies daily by 1913, most of it shared by five popular papers: *Le Journal*, *Le Petit Journal*, *Le Matin*, *Le Petit Parisien* and *L'Echo de Paris*. German newspapers remained relatively conservative

PRINT SUPPLIER The British chain, W.H. Smith, both supplied and stimulated the appetite for news.

in the years before the First World War. They were also decentralised; the principal newspapers of Hamburg, Frankfurt or Munich were just as influential as any published in Berlin. No German paper reached sales of 1 million copies, as was achieved in London and Paris, but the well-educated German public supported nearly 3000 different daily or weekly papers.

THE READING HABIT

The flood of cheap reading material for the newly literate, whether in the form of newspapers, magazines or books, was a source of concern to many educated observers of the time. It had been hoped that compulsory elementary education

---

AN AMERICAN HABIT

The first chewing-gum vending machines were installed in stations on the New York elevated railroad in 1888. They sold Tutti-Frutti gum. Americans had been chewing gum made from chicle (the juice of the sapodilla tree) since the 1870s, but efforts to market it in Europe were unsuccessful. When Wrigleys first introduced its gum into Britain in 1911, sweetshops refused to stock it, and it was available only from vending machines.

---

would raise the cultural level of 'the masses'. But the new readers wanted entertainment rather than enlightenment, and the popular publishers of the day were quick to recognise and exploit this fact. Millions of young men and women emerging from the elementary schools simply wanted 'something to read'. When life and work for most of them was drab and monotonous, the popular novel, newspaper or magazine serial offered an escape into a brighter world.

When these new readers combined their numbers with a middle-class readership also in search of entertainment rather than serious literature, the phenomenon of the 'best seller' – selling 1 million or more copies over a short time – was born. In the English-speaking world before the First World War, the best sellers included Jack London's *The Call of the Wild* (1903), Baroness Orczy's *The Scarlet Pimpernel* (1905), Elinor Glyn's scandalous *Three Weeks* (1907), Jeffrey Farnol's *The Broad Highway* (1910), Ethel M. Dell's *The Way of an Eagle* (1912) and Edgar Rice Burroughs' *Tarzan of the Apes* (1914).

Some of the 20th-century writers most admired today – Rainer Maria Rilke, André Gide, Marcel Proust, James Joyce, D.H. Lawrence and Thomas Mann – were already at work in the years before the First World War, but none of them came near to approaching the status of a best seller.

THE RISE OF THE CINEMA

The rise of the cinema rivals in its suddenness the emergence of the motor car, which occurred at almost exactly the same time. Credit for cinema's invention generally goes to the Frenchmen Auguste and Louis Lumière, whose *cinématographe* was first demonstrated at the Grand Café in the Boulevard des Capucines, Paris, in 1895.

At first, the experience merely of seeing moving images on a screen was sensational enough. The earliest films lasted only a minute or two, and showed exotic views, sporting events, or circus or
(continued on page 124)

LIGHT MAGIC The *cinématographe* seemed an exciting miracle, both to its practitioners, like this German cameraman of 1912, and (inset) to the first cinema audiences, who were stunned by films lasting only a minute or two.

CINÉMATOGRAPHE LUMIÈRE

ON THE SET

The cinema was born in the 1890s, and only a few years later it was an industry big and profitable enough to justify the building of studios like this one belonging to the Edison Company in New York, in which several films could be made simultaneously. Sunlight was unreliable as a light source, so mercury-vapour lamps provided a diffuse and even light. Early cameras had limited depth of field so the action had to take place close to the lens, and the direction of most films owed more to the theatre than to the freer potential of the new medium. Since the films were silent, there was no problem in filming a Western shoot-out and a domestic drama at the same time, while workmen prepared another set, and actors rehearsed for another film. Studios like this could produce several short films in the course of a week. Before long, however, the American movie industry moved to the benign climate and spectacular scenery of California, and Hollywood became synonymous with popular film-making.

QUO VADIS"

A First National Picture

At the voluptuous court of Caesar

CINEMA MILESTONES
Edwin S. Porter's *The Great Train Robbery* (1903), which demonstrated film's special power to tell a story, was one of the cinema's first masterpieces; *Quo Vadis* (1912) was one of the earliest epic spectaculars. Charlie Chaplin, a film-making genius, was among the first film-stars.

vaudeville acts; they formed just part of the entertainment in music-halls or in tent-shows, which otherwise consisted of live acts. Only gradually did film-makers begin to introduce actors in order to produce short dramatic or comedy films.

At this early stage, European film-makers were doing more exciting things with the new medium than those in the USA. In France, for example, Georges Méliès was producing brilliant science fantasy films in the early 1900s, and actors from the *Comédie Française* were brought in to play in French films. Italy was producing costume dramas and Biblical epics. Until 1908 nearly half the films shown in New York were imported from Europe.

From 1905, cinemas dedicated solely to the showing of moving pictures were being opened, and proved hugely popular and profitable for their owners. Admission was cheap, only 5 cents in the USA and 1d in Britain, where they were known as 'penny gaffs'. One of the first films shown in them was *The Great Train Robbery* by the American Edwin S. Porter. By 1910, there were 10 000 such cinemas in the USA alone, and it was estimated that on average they were visited by over 2 million

people – one-third of them children – every day of the year. In 1907, an American journalist described the early cinemas:

'The nickelodeon is usually a tiny theatre, containing 199 seats, giving twelve to eighteen performances a day, seven days a week. Its walls are painted red. The seats are ordinary kitchen chairs, not fastened. The only break in the red colour scheme is made by half a dozen signs, in black and white, No Smoking, Hats Off and sometimes, but not always, Stay as Long as You Like. Last year or the year before it was probably a second-hand clothier's, a pawnshop or cigar store. Now the counter has been ripped out, there's a ticket-seller's booth where the show-window was, an automatic musical barker somewhere up in the air thunders its noise down on the passer-by, and the little store has been converted into a theatrelet. Not a theatre, mind you, for theatres must take out theatrical licences at 500 dollars a year. Theatres sit two hundred or more people. Nickelodeons seat 199, and take out amusement licences.'

SMILE PLEASE

In 1889 the Eastman Company began manufacturing the first Celluloid roll film for use in their new Kodak cameras. The availability of inexpensive, easy-to-use cameras made photography a popular hobby for the first time since its invention. From the 1890s onwards, ordinary people could begin to 'snap' each other and the world about them.

LIVE THEATRE Despite the rise of the cinema, a visit to the Vienna State Opera was as popular as ever. Right: Prince Charming, from Cinderella, was one of the many heroes and heroines that helped the traditional English pantomime to flourish.

By 1912, the early 'nickelodeons' were giving way to larger movie theatres, many of them able to seat 1000 or more spectators. By 1913, a financial report for the German city of Hanover showed that income from the amusement tax on the cinema exceeded the combined receipts from the city's theatres and variety halls. With this assured market, the film companies now began to set up studios, hire companies of actors on a permanent basis and produce longer narrative films lasting about 15 minutes. Australia, for example, produced *The Story of the Ned Kelly Gang* in 1910. And in 1912, Mack Sennett and his Keystone comedy team started making films in Hollywood, which grew rapidly as a film-making centre from 1906 onwards.

The First World War, which brought the development of the European cinema to a halt, gave Hollywood the chance to become pre-eminent. Before America entered the war in 1917, the American director D.W. Griffith had produced his two mammoth spectacular epics, *The Birth of a Nation* (1915) and

Intolerance (1916), with their casts of thousands and gigantic sets.

A mere 20 years after its birth, the cinema was a familiar part of everyday life. Hollywood already had its 'stars', such as Douglas Fairbanks, Mary Pickford and Charlie Chaplin, and a worldwide common culture had been created. Chaplin introduced his 'little tramp' character in 1914; the comic walk he developed for that role was to be imitated by soldiers on both sides in the First World War.

THE LIVELY ARTS

The rise of the cinema, somewhat looked down upon by the educated classes in its early years, had little or no effect on the popularity of the theatre in the period before the First World War. The theatre

SUPERSTAR The French actress Sarah Bernhardt joined the *Comédie Française* in 1866 and dominated the world stage for half a century, even after her right leg was amputated in 1915.

A VISIT TO THE PANTOMIME

A visit to the theatre in the years around 1900 was a very special experience for a child. Ernest Shepard describes his first visit to the pantomime, at London's Drury Lane Theatre.

❛ At last we reached Long Acre and, turning into Drury Lane, came in sight of the gas torches burning under the great portico of the theatre.... We left our cab and, struggling through the press of people and clinging to each other, made our way up the steps....

Waiting while Father fumbled for the tickets was misery.... Suppose he had lost them! Or suppose they were for the wrong day! But all was well, and we crowded inside and along the passage, where a woman in an apron opened a small door and we were shown into our box There the full glory of the place burst upon us. I stood

looking at the auditorium.... Somebody brought a programme and the orchestra began to tune up. Then the great circle of gas in the roof was turned up and the limelights in the wings began to fizz. A general hush descended on the audience. Threading his way among the orchestra came the conductor.... Then the curtain rose and I became lost to all around me, translated to another land, borne aloft on magic wings into another world.... I remember a gay young woman with prominent teeth and a flaxen wig who sang and danced bewitchingly. She could only have been Marie Lloyd, the unforgettable, aged seventeen and in her first Pantomime at "the Lane"....

It was all such a feast of colour, music and fun, and it would be quite impossible to express all the emotions that were aroused in a

small boy's breast. I know that I stood gripping the velvet-covered front of the box, lost in a wonderful dream....

The spectacle reached a climax with the transformation scene. Glittering vistas appeared one behind the other, sparkling lace-like canopies spread overhead, a real fountain poured forth in the background. On either side golden brackets swung out from the wings, each with its reclining nymph, solid and spangled and in a graceful attitude. Flying fairies, poised but swaying gently, filled the air and formed a sort of triumphal archway, below which the performers gathered. The Good Fairy, stepping forward, invoked in rhymed couplets the Spirit of Pantomime, and out from the wings burst Joey the clown, Pantaloon, Columbine and Harlequin to complete the tableau. ❜

in late Victorian and Edwardian England was dominated by Oscar Wilde (before his fall from grace), James Barrie, George Bernard Shaw, Arthur Wing Pinero and John Galsworthy, who was also to achieve great success with his novel sequence, *The Forsyte Saga*. Shaw's plays were being produced almost continuously in England from 1905 onwards and were also put on in Paris, Berlin and New York. German audiences were receptive to foreign plays and enjoyed the work of

Shaw, Henrik Ibsen, August Strindberg and Anton Chekhov as well as that of German-language playwrights such as Gerhart Hauptmann, Frank Wedekind and Arthur Schnitzler.

Many of these playwrights dealt in a rather

MOULIN ROUGE The cabaret was the Paris equivalent of the British music hall, and was celebrated by Henri de Toulouse-Lautrec in a series of paintings and drawings.

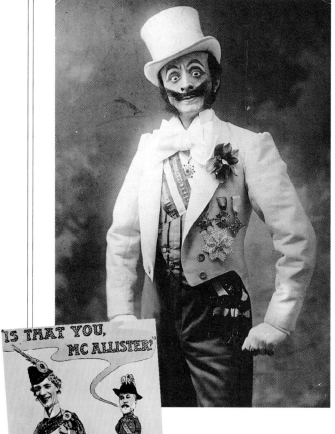

HARRY LAUDER.

STAGE PRESENCE **The music-hall artiste dominated audiences through sheer personality and the power of his voice. The Scottish singer and songwriter Harry Lauder (inset) was one of the most successful.**

the workhouse from his beloved wife of 40 years, while 'My Old Man Said Follow the Van' describes a couple moving all their possessions in a cart because they can no longer pay the rent.

Music-hall artistes such as Marie Lloyd, Charles Coborn, Albert Chevalier and Harry Lauder could earn fortunes, and, through their appearance on the covers of sheet music as well as through their live performances, became stars in their own country. In an age before microphones, they mastered the art of projecting their voices and their personalities to the remotest seats in the gallery. The variety format enabled them to perform in several places on the same evening, dashing from one, music hall to another in cabs. The best of them had complete control over their audiences, who could otherwise be rowdy, especially since the music halls were well provided with bars and had long been associated with heavy drinking. When the gramophone came into use, several music-hall artistes were among the first to be recorded.

American vaudeville was much influenced by the British music hall. In return, the USA sent Britain its minstrel shows, in which white singers and musicians blacked up their faces and performed sentimental songs about life on the cotton plantation; such shows were immensely popular in late Victorian England and introduced British audiences to the American singer, Eugene

sombre fashion with the social and moral issues of the day. As light relief, Vienna gave to the rest of the world the escapist joys of the operetta. Johann Strauss the Younger's *Die Fledermaus* and Franz Lehar's *The Merry Widow* still seem to sum up for many the gaiety and charm of the *belle epoque*.

Outside the world of the 'respectable' drama, other forms of live theatre were enjoying a period of remarkable vigour. The English music hall and its American equivalent, vaudeville, were at the height of their success as a robustly popular form of entertainment. They offered a variety of acts, announced by a master of ceremonies and dominated by the comic or sentimental song. The performers came almost entirely from the urban working class and their songs, however comical, often reflected the realities of working-class life: in 'My Old Dutch', for example, an elderly man contemplates the prospect of being separated in

HIS MASTER'S VOICE **Music-hall entertainers took advantage of the gramophone to record their work.**

In the older dances, the upper body was held still and the dancers held each other at arm's length, if they touched at all. The new dances involved close bodily contact and not merely violent movements of the legs, but also agitated motions of the female bosom and hips that were regarded as highly suggestive and were much frowned upon by an older generation. The new dance steps were demonstrated by the Britons Vernon and Irene Castle, who also danced in the USA, and by Gaby Deslys in Paris.

The USA had already developed the song-publishing industry that came to be known as Tin Pan Alley. It had created a distinctively American popular music style, influenced by black musical traditions, but dominated by composers who were recent immigrants from Central and Eastern Europe. This new music greatly influenced Europe, whereas in the 1890s it was European operetta and musical comedy that had flowed towards the USA. Before the arrival, in large numbers, of the gramophone or phonograph, the new music spread through sales of sheet music, which reached a peak in the 1910s with annual sales of around 200 million copies, many of them selling through stores such as Woolworth's. Dance tunes were in great demand, producing huge sellers like Irving Berlin's 'Alexander's Ragtime Band' (1911), but sentimental ballads were even more popular.

Sheet music only gradually gave way to gramophone records, although the latter were on sale from the 1890s. The American Victrola record-player was manufactured for domestic use from 1906, but widespread use of the gramophone began only with the arrival of the portable gramophone in 1913. The Decca Portable was to become almost standard equipment in the trenches of the Western Front during the First World War.

BALLET REVOLUTION The ballets of Sergei Diaghilev and the Ballets Russes, such as *L'Après Midi d'un Faune* and *The Firebird* (right), shocked traditional audiences.

Stratton. Stratton's songs, which included the hugely successful 'Lily of Laguna', were actually written by an Englishman from Lancashire, Leslie Stuart.

America also exported to Britain and Europe the syncopated rhythms of ragtime and the cakewalk. Europeans loved the new music, without having much awareness that it had developed from the work of black composers such as Scott Joplin. From about 1910, they developed a passion for dancing, which now increasingly took place in public, in dance halls, cabarets, restaurants and hotels, as well as at private parties.

BALLET GENIUS

Vaslav Nijinsky, possibly the greatest of all ballet dancers, became an international sensation when he performed with Diaghilev's Ballets Russes between 1909 and 1917. He seemed to defy gravity by pausing in midair at the peak of his leaps. He suffered a breakdown in 1919 and died in 1950.

SPORTS AND GAMES

Increasing numbers of people, including women, began to participate in sports, and to attend sporting events as spectators, for the first time. And governing bodies and rules for most games were established by the early 1900s.

THE EARLY 1900s were a period notable for the rise of popular professional and spectator sports and for their growing internationalisation.

Association football (soccer), whose rules had been developed in the British public schools during the first half of the 19th century and taught to working-class boys in the clubs that the schools organised for them in the cities, had by the end of the century become the favourite working-class spectator sport in Britain, with professional teams based mainly on the industrial towns. It had also spread to the rest of the world. It reached Denmark in the 1880s, and sailors and businessmen introduced it into Brazil and Russia. Austria and Hungary played their first international match in 1902. In 1904 Belgium, Denmark, France, Holland,

CUP FEVER In the 1905 Football Association Cup Final, a packed crowd watches as Aston Villa beat Newcastle United by two goals to nil.

AMATEUR ATHLETICS The Yale University track team of 1899 was among many that sought sporting success.

Spain, Sweden and Switzerland formed the game's international governing body, FIFA (*Fédération Internationale de Football Association*), which Britain did not join until 1946.

By 1910 there were some 12 000 football clubs registered with the British Football Association and cup finals were being played out before vast crowds – 120 000 at the FA Cup Final in 1913. The major football teams, now almost entirely professional, were increasingly run as profitable businesses. Popular newspapers throughout the Western world were covering sport of all kinds, and in 1900 there were 25 London newspapers devoted entirely to sport.

Increased prosperity and changing work patterns gave people more time for sport. Interest in football, in following favoured teams and star players, had come to dominate working-class life in Britain and in many of the industrial cities of Europe also. But interest in spectator sports generally was on the increase; there were long queues, for example, for the Wimbledon Men's Final in 1913.

Association football also spread to the USA, but failed to prevail there over the rugby-based version

CATCH! **Baseball remained the American national game.**

of the game. Australia, too, preferred its own unique version, in which the ball might be kicked or punched and carried for a few yards, but not thrown. American football was still college-based and dominated by Ivy League schools such as Harvard, Princeton and Yale. The players wore small leather helmets or no helmets at all, but it was a rough game. In the 1900s its rules were regularly re-written to make it safer and more interesting, and tactically more subtle. This seemed especially necessary after the season of 1905, in which it was estimated that 18 deaths and 159 major injuries had resulted from college games, and as a result of

SUMMER SPORTS **The lawn tennis championships at Wimbledon were a favourite spectator sport by 1914. Inset: Mrs Lambert Chambers in action in the Ladies' Singles Final on her way to victory over Ethel Larcome.**

which President Theodore Roosevelt had summoned college representatives and urged them to save the game by eliminating 'brutality and foul play'.

College football already had its heroes, such as Hobey Baker and 'Buzz' Law, but it did not as yet have wide popular appeal. Twenty-thousand people watched the Yale-Harvard game of November 1900, but that was regarded as an exceptionally large crowd. The *New York Times* reported on the game that 'the society and club worlds of this city exhibited an intense interest in

---

EYEWITNESS

CYCLING TO THE MATCH

H.C.A. Harrison was an early player of Australian Rules football, a cricket fan, and a cyclist. In the summer of 1896, aged 62, he set out to ride the 600 miles (965 km) from Melbourne to Sydney to attend a test match.

❝ The journey took me nine and a half days, travelling on an average of 63 miles [100 km] a day. I followed the old Sydney Road, which I had not travelled over since my babyhood, and then under very different circumstances. Instead of a rough track through the bush, there was a hard metalled road a good part of the way, and instead of camping in tents or waggons on the wayside every night, I was able to put up at some quite comfortable inns. Instead of being on my guard

against attacks by blacks, all I saw of them were two poor old fellows from a neighbouring mission station, whom I met while sitting on the verandah of a hotel, where I happened to be lunching, about 100 miles (160 km) from Sydney, and with whom I had a long and friendly "yabber"....

I passed through Albury, calling on a few relations and old friends there, and then on through Germanton, Goulburn, Moss Vale, and Picton . . . Picton is about 60 miles (95 km) from Sydney, and I felt, on leaving there, that my effort was practically over. But, strange to say, I had my first accident after negotiating the (then) difficult road over Razorback. I ran into a stump and twisted the pedal just before reaching Minto. Fortunately an

obliging blacksmith was able to straighten it out for me. The bicycle, by the way, was an Elswick, very strongly and solidly built, with rubber tyres, but had no free wheel at the time. I afterwards had one put on.

On arriving at Strathfield I left the bicycle to be repaired. At about 8 o'clock in the evening I took a tram into Sydney, and put up at the Hotel Australia, where the cricketers were. I was greeted with surprise by them all, as they had predicted that I would break down before getting half-way, and be obliged to finish the journey by train. Prince Ranjitsinhji added his congratulations to the others and said: "I should think, Mr Harrison, that this ride, for a man of your age, must be a world's record." ❞

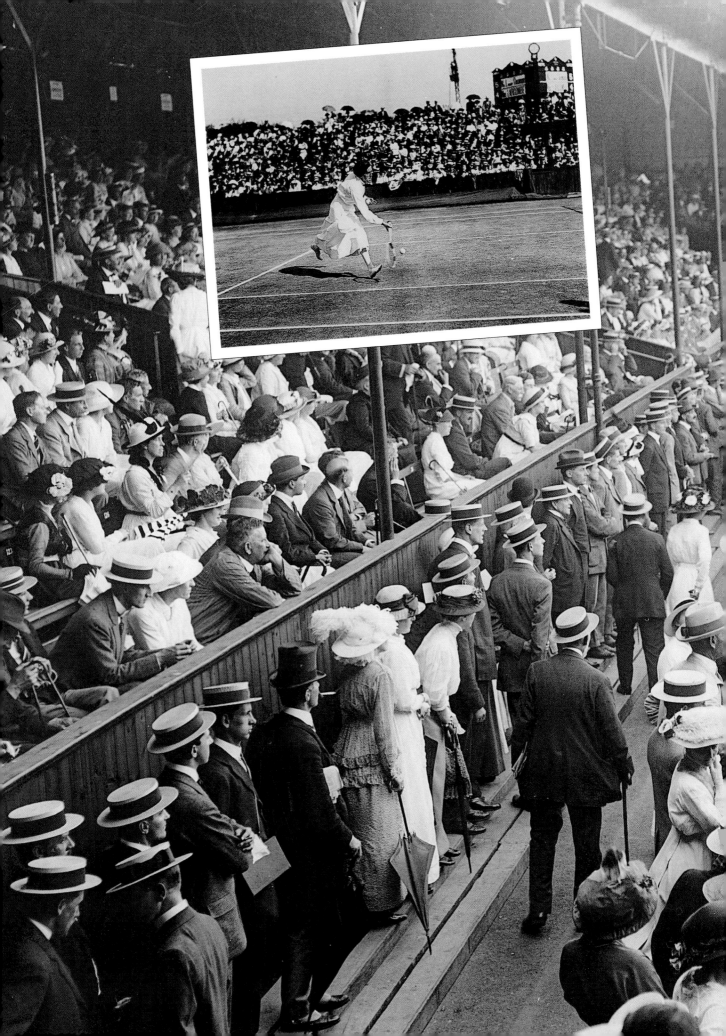

WITH THE GLOVES ON

The first world heavyweight championship fought with gloves on the boxers' hands took place in Cincinnati in 1885. John L. Sullivan of the United States defeated his fellow Irish-American Dominick McCaffery for the title.

yesterday's game' and went on to suggest that 'to give a list of the well-known men and women present would be to reprint whole pages of the Social Register'.

Organised games that required special costumes and equipment were regarded by most Americans as belonging to the world of the rich of the Eastern cities. Golf had reached Chicago in 1893, but was played mainly by wealthy Easterners, as was tennis, for which the annual US Championships were held in the rich people's resort of Newport, Rhode Island.

Basketball was only invented in 1892. Baseball, whose modern rules had been established during the Civil War, was the truly popular American game. Its major league players had been professionals since the 1870s, but it was a game that needed only a sand-lot and the minimum of equipment and was played everywhere by Americans of all classes.

GENTLEMEN AND PLAYERS

In Britain, association football apart, the amateur ethos was still strong and strictly enforced. The ethos was influenced by the team sports that were compulsory in the British public schools, emphasising 'fair play', limiting aggression and 'forming

SPORTSMEN Rugby football was an amateur game, played at schools and universities. The British sporting ethos spread throughout the Empire; this West Indian cricket team of 1906 (inset) was the second to visit Britain.

AMATEURS AND PROFESSIONALS An exhausted Dorando Pietri breaks the finishing tape in the marathon at the 1908 Olympics. However, he was disqualified for being helped over the line. Right: Jack Johnson, the first black world heavyweight champion, knocks out former title-holder Jim Jeffries in 1910.

character' as well as working off energy that might otherwise be channelled in undesirable ways. In cricket, a clear distinction was made between 'gentlemen' amateurs and paid professionals, who might play together but would have separate dressing rooms.

In the last years of the 19th century, Britain led the world in codifying the rules of different games and sports – cricket, rugby football, boxing, lawn tennis, hockey, golf, badminton – and then exported them to most of the rest of the world.

DRESSED FOR COMFORT Women abandoned their corsets and bustles, and wore stylish, practical clothes, like this French golfing outfit of 1912, for sporting activities.

In the 1900s, international sporting associations were being formed – for lawn tennis, for example, in 1913. The International Olympic Committee, for international competition in athletics of all kinds, had been founded in 1895, and the first modern Olympic Games took place in the following year. From the start, athletics events were dominated by competitors from the United States, who in the Games of 1904 won all but two of the 23 track and field titles.

The Olympic Committee stressed the amateur principle, and most of those who took part in the Olympic Games in the years before the First World War were men from well-to-do backgrounds. Many sports were still socially exclusive. Golf (other than in Scotland) and tennis were limited almost entirely to the middle and upper classes, as was skiing, a sport that had recently become fashionable.

At the same time, concern about the general level of fitness of the population led to the encouragement

When Johnson retained his heavyweight title against Jim Jeffries in 1910, his win provoked race riots.

SPORTING WOMEN

Sport was largely dominated by men. Women were barred by the Olympic Committee from taking part in gymnastics and track and field events, although they participated in some events at the Olympic Games of 1900, where Britain's Charlotte Cooper was the first woman ever to win an Olympic gold medal, for the women's tennis singles. In the 1904 Games, women competed only in archery. In the Olympics of 1908, 36 women participated – in tennis, archery, figure-skating and yachting – compared with over 2000 male athletes.

Tennis, figure-skating and golf were among the few sports regarded as suitable for women. Hockey, netball and lacrosse were played in girls' schools and colleges, but strictly separated from the rougher men's versions. However, young women were growing increasingly interested in sport, and looser, less-restricting clothing was being developed so that they could take part.

Cycling was one recreation in which both sexes and all classes could participate. The development of the pneumatic-tyred bicycle, with chain-transmission from the pedals to the rear wheel, had taken place at the end of the 1880s, making cycling comfortable, safe and relatively effortless. Bicycles also became much cheaper. In the USA

of some sports among working-class boys. One of the most popular was boxing, whose rules had been established in the 1880s. In London's East End, Father Osborne Jay, vicar of Shoreditch, was an enthusiastic patron of working-class boxing. In the USA, professional boxing in the 1900s offered a way out of poverty for the sons of poor immigrants and for young black boys such as Jack Johnson, who was to become world champion despite strong prejudice against black fighters.

FREEDOM RIDERS Bicycling necessitated a change in women's fashions from long skirts and large hats to something more practical.

they cost between $100 and $150 in 1893; by 1901 the price was only $15. In Britain, by 1894 a new bicycle could be bought for as little as £4.50, a sum that a working man could make up in saved public transport fares in less than a year. Nonetheless, the bicycle was one of the most expensive pieces of property that most families of the time owned.

Tricycles were still being made for adults in considerable numbers – Queen Victoria owned several herself. Tandems were also much favoured, leading to the 1892 song 'Daisy Bell', popular on both sides of the Atlantic,

LEVELLER British socialists pose before setting off on their bicycles. The bicycle obscured the line between those who did and did not ride horses. By 1908, as this German catalogue shows (inset), it had reached its modern form.

THE WILDEST GAME

ALMOST ALL the games played internationally have their origins in games played in the British Isles. Two exceptions are polo and lacrosse. Polo was played in Persia at least 2000 years ago and came to the West by way of India, where it had been taken up by British tea-planters and army officers. In the 1870s it reached the USA, where the Polo Association, which standardised the rules, was formed in 1890.

Lacrosse was originally a game played by the Six Nations of the Iroquois of North America. In their version of the game, called 'baggataway', as many as 1000 players took part, the goals were miles apart, and a game might last three days. The lacrosse stick was used to disable as many opposing players as possible as well as to catch and propel the ball. Because it bore some resemblance to a bishop's crozier, French settlers called it *la crosse*.

The white Canadians modified

HORSEPLAY Polo, one of the world's oldest games, was taken up by the very rich. Here, England play Ireland at Hurlingham in 1910.

the rules somewhat, reducing the number of players to 12 on each side, and lacrosse, officially declared Canada's national game, spread to the USA, England, Australia and New Zealand. It was included in the Olympic Games of 1904 and 1908, but has never achieved popularity outside the English-speaking world.

SKI STYLE In the 1900s, skiing rapidly became a popular recreational sport among the wealthy.

about 'a bicycle built for two'.

The first races for bicycles with pneumatic tyres took place in France in 1891. In the same year the first bicycle race-tracks were built in Paris and New York. At the first six-day race on the New York track, competitors used the older type of bicycle with the front wheel much bigger than the rear and they had to ride the entire race themselves; the winner was the

American, Charlie Miller, who covered 2093 miles (3368 km) in the six days. This was too exhausting for most cyclists, and team relay races were introduced in 1894.

The Tour de France was inaugurated in 1903. It was contested in six stages over 1510 miles (2430 km), the route taking in Paris, Lyon, Marseilles, Toulouse, Bordeaux and Nantes. The race took 19 days, and out of 60 competitors who started, only 22 completed the course, Maurice Garin being the winner. The Tour de France was run annually, and the races of the early years were won mainly by riders from France, Belgium and Italy, the countries that have dominated the sport ever since.

THE PLEASURES OF SOCIETY

Hunting, shooting and fishing were still the preferred sports of the ruling classes,

although yachting and horse racing were also becoming popular. Among the diversions

of the rich, bridge and flirtation also played their parts.

THE KILLING GAME   A rhinoceros is the trophy of these big-game hunters in Africa.

THE PROUD ENGLISH peer Lord Redesdale once informed his children that only the middle classes played games – gentlemen took part in sport. By sport he meant hunting, shooting and fishing, still the dominant activities of the ruling classes everywhere. The American president, Theodore Roosevelt, was an intrepid sportsman in this sense. Edward, Prince of Wales, later King Edward VII – although he also adored more urban pleasures – based a large part of his year on shooting deer and grouse at Balmoral and feathered game of all kinds at Sandringham. Officers in the British army welcomed service abroad for the opportunities it gave them to shoot duck in Egypt or tigers in India.

By the 1890s Kenya had become a favourite resort of big-game hunters from Europe and North America, offering the pleasure of slaughtering elephants, lions and giraffes. Closer to home, some of the grandest hunting of all took place on the great estates of Germany and the Austro-Hungarian Empire, where wild boar and other large

COMPLEAT ANGLER
A fisherman in the
costume favoured by
the royal household at
Balmoral.

THE CARRIAGE AWAITS This country house in the Brandenburg area of Germany was built around 1900, and is typical of houses being built at the time by those who had recently become members of the landowning class. Inset: In Britain, fox-hunting was a pleasure pursued by rich and not-so-rich alike.

game could still be hunted, and the wealthy estate owners employed a permanent staff of liveried huntsmen who not only assisted at the hunt but could also entertain guests with music on their hunting horns.

For many of the British aristocracy, fox-hunting was a consuming passion, as it was also in the USA for the landed gentry of New England and Virginia. The Duke of Portland estimated that over a period of 15 years he had had at least two days' hunting a week with 26 different packs of hounds, and Lord Willoughby de Broke declared that 'hunting four times a week for seven months of the year is not a profession that affords much leisure for entertaining'. The passion was shared by many women, among them Winston Churchill's mother, Lady Randolph Churchill, and Margot Asquith, who hunted even while pregnant. It was one of the few sports that gave women an opportunity to compete with men on equal terms and to demonstrate courage as well as skill. Nor was it entirely socially exclusive, for in hunting country many farmers took part, in the interest of controlling the fox population.

IN THE BAG

In the late 19th and early 20th centuries, there was considerable tension in the countryside between huntsmen and shooting estates, since, in 'shooting counties', gamekeepers were frequently accused

THE MEN'S ROOM The German hunting lodge preserved a medieval and totally masculine atmosphere.

of poisoning foxes in order to protect the birds. Shooting was at the peak of its popularity in those years. Every country mansion had its gunroom, its walls adorned with antlers and glass cases of stuffed fish and racks of guns. The nobility of Germany and Austro-Hungary had their hunting lodges, furnished in a similar way, where the men could spend days, or even weeks, in masculine comfort while they pursued the local game.

Keeping a shooting estate was an expensive business. A popular saying of the time was: 'Up gets a guinea, bang goes a penny halfpenny, and down comes half-a-crown'; it referred respectively to the cost of rearing the pheasant, the price of the cartridge that shot it, and the market value of the bird when dead, and meant in effect that each bird shot had cost the landowner about £1.

The Earl of Crawford complained about the increasing cost of hiring beaters on Scottish estates: 'One now pays five shillings a day to these youths, and into the bargain they have to be driven to the moor . . . (but) when the last increase in wages was conceded, their free lunch was knocked off, which is considered a real advantage, as the boys now bring their own frugal bread and cheese with them whereas previously they gorged themselves at their employers' expense.'

Because of the high cost of preserving game, landlords feared the activities of poachers. By 1901

LIVING IT UP The huge fortune of the American Astor family was recently acquired, but their lifestyle was one of the grandest and most lavish in the world.

THE JOYS OF SMOKING

IN THE YEARS around 1900, most men smoked. The wealthy smoked Havana cigars; humbler Europeans smoked cheaper cigars from the East Indies; but the majority of middle and working-class smokers favoured the pipe.

Cigarettes originated in Turkey and Russia, and it is probable that their use spread to Western Europe after the Crimean War. Turkish and Russian cigarettes had been hand-rolled, as were the earliest cigarettes made in the West – a trained worker could fill about 1250 paper tubes in a day – but machine-rolling was well established by the 1870s. In Britain, brands such as Gold Flake, Woodbine, Weights and Player's Navy Cut were introduced in the 1880s and 1890s. Cigarettes were sold in soft paper packets and easily crushed; the practice of including a cardboard stiffener in the packet led to the introduction of cigarette cards. The first cigarettes to appear in cardboard packets were Wills' Three Castles in 1892.

Cigarette-smoking was not as yet a popular habit, but was increasingly taken up by wealthy sophisticates in the 1890s. They, however, favoured Turkish or Egyptian cigarettes to the Virginia tobacco of the cheaper brands. Gentlemen bought their cigarettes by weight rather than in packets, and carried them in cigarette cases.

In respectable society, women did not smoke in public. In 1896,

THE POLITICS OF SMOKING Members of a mainly female group of the 1890s smoke rather self-consciously, as a gesture of liberation. Below: Cigarette advertisements emphasised the serenity and reflectiveness engendered by tobacco.

the Duchesse de Clermont-Tonnerre created a sensation by lighting up a cigarette in the dining room of the Savoy Hotel in London. By that time, women were quite commonly smoking cigarettes or small cigars in the privacy of their own rooms – it was claimed in the women's magazine *Home Companion* in 1897 that no fewer than six European queens were smokers (Victoria was not one of them).

In 1897 the *Southern Tobacco Journal* of Richmond, Virginia, published an advertisement showing a woman smoking a cigarette, but the experiment was not repeated until 1919. In 1908, the City of New York made it an indictable offence for a woman to smoke in public.

It was the First World War that popularised the practice of cigarette-smoking, as cigarettes were more convenient to carry and light in the stressful conditions of trench warfare. The war also led to a great increase in public smoking by women.

A PASSION FOR RACING Crowds gather around the totalisator at Chantilly, one of France's most fashionable racecourses. Inset: At Eton school, boat crews process down the river before the races begin, while proud parents look on.

nearly 17 000 gamekeepers were employed on estates in England, heavily outnumbering policemen in country districts. Nevertheless, the high cost of the sport did not deter enthusiasts, for whom a day's shooting combined good sport with an agreeable social occasion.

Great pride was taken in the sheer size of the 'bag'. At one four-day shooting party on the Prince of Wales's Sandringham estate, for example, nine or ten guns between them took 4135 pheasants, 2009 partridges, 232 hares, 576 rabbits, 14 woodcock, 275 wild duck, 12 pigeons, and 3 unspecified 'various'. The partridge 'bag' on the last day was 1342, a Sandringham record. At the end of the morning's shooting, one of the prince's equerries would ask each of the guests how many birds he had shot. The figures were then read out at lunch, much to the embarrassment of those who had done badly.

In England, certain people were recognised as outstanding shots by the shooting fraternity. They included the Duke of York (later King George V) and Lord de Grey. The latter was estimated to have killed more than $1/2$ million birds in a shooting career of just over 50 years. On one occasion he was seen to kill 52 birds with 54 shots, 'and for a bet this was done with one hand', using three guns and two loaders, men who re-loaded his guns for him. In the fashion of the time, he liked to claim that he achieved these feats effortlessly, but on one occasion a fellow guest came downstairs at night to find him in the library with his two loaders, practising his gun-changing. He was not pleased to be discovered.

WAITING FOR THE MEN

A few women, including the Duchess of Bedford and the Comtesse de Paris, became expert shots, but shooting was mainly a sport for men, and many wives found a shooting weekend a tedious and uneventful business.

The Countess of Warwick remembered: 'The

A GAME TO ENLIVEN THE EVENING

THE GAME of bridge, which enlivened the evenings of many households from the 1890s onwards, probably originated in Turkey. The first rules of the game were certainly compiled there by an Englishman, John Collinson, who published a pamphlet about the game on his return to England in 1886, although there is some evidence that it had been played among the Greek community in Manchester as early as the 1870s.

In 1892 bridge arrived in New York, where it immediately became popular. In 1894, Lord Brougham, who had learned the game in Cairo, introduced it to the Portland Club, and within a matter of months it

had ousted whist as the favourite game of the London clubs and was becoming equally popular at country-house weekends

The version of the game known as auction bridge is said to have been invented by three Anglo-Indians, who found themselves without a fourth player at their remote hill-station in 1902. The rules for four-handed play were established in 1906. Contract bridge was also devised in India, at Poona in 1912, and the first rules were published in the *Times of India* in 1914, but this version of the game did not catch on in Europe and North America until the 1920s.

CONSIDERING HER HAND Bridge became a fashionable pastime among the leisured classes.

men went out shooting after breakfast and then came the emptiness of the long morning from which I suffered silently. I can remember the groups of women sitting discussing their neighbours or writing letters at impossible little ornamental tables. . . . We were not all women. There were a few unsporting men asked – "darlings".

PORT AND CIGARS After dinner, the women withdrew and the gentlemen stayed behind in the dining room for serious talk.

These men of witty and amusing conversation were always asked everywhere as extras to help to entertain the women; otherwise we should have been left high and dry.'

Most women joined the shooting party for luncheon and then returned to the house to wait for the men's return at tea time. The shoot continued in the afternoon, but, for all but the most dedicated, the luncheon effectively ended serious shooting for the day, for it was almost invariably a lavish and substantial affair, especially if the Prince of Wales was involved.

Those who had to entertain the prince on their own estates found it an expensive business – one peer estimated that having royalty at his house for a week might cost between £5000 and £10 000. Yet the prestige attached to having royalty as guests was such that several families were prepared to get into debt in order to do so. In one extreme case, Lord Walsingham was ruined by the experience of entertaining Edward regularly. In the 1890s he lent the prince one of his estates for a year's shooting, and at the expiry of the lease found that the wine cellar his family had filled over generations had been emptied. In 1912 he was obliged to sell a substantial part of his lands, including valuable real estate in London. Eventually he was forced to live abroad.

FLIRTATION AND OTHER PLEASURES

Shooting ended with the failing light, and guests at a country-house weekend then had to seek other amusements. Between tea and 7 o'clock, when guests went up to change for dinner, card-playing served to relieve the tedium, but flirtation was also a favourite amusement. Among the 'fast set' around the Prince of Wales, hostesses discreetly allocated bedrooms so that amorous liaisons could be conducted at night; the 2nd Duke of Westminster advised that it was wise when thus engaged 'to walk on the outside of the staircase, as it creaked less, and never to touch the bannisters as one surreptitiously crept upstairs'.

But the English country-house weekend also offered more innocent pleasures. In the summer, many houses arranged cricket matches, some of them involving first-class players, others informal affairs at which guests took on teams from the local village. Many houses offered the chance to fish, or to play croquet, tennis or golf, a game that became increasingly popular in the early 1900s.

For the British upper class, the social year also included the major race meetings at Newmarket,

Ascot, Sandown, Goodwood, Doncaster and Epsom, the Eton and Harrow cricket match, and Henley regatta. Ascot and Henley, in particular, were important social occasions, on which correct dress and rigid social distinctions were given more attention than the racing itself.

For the 'fast set', racing involved gambling, sometimes on a massive scale. Several members of the aristocracy were addicted to it. The 8th Marquess of Queensbury and his brother were said to have lost more than £700 000 on gambling ventures of various kinds, and the Prince of Wales himself was touched by scandal arising from gambling at the illegal game of baccarat. At their clubs, men would gamble at cards or on the results of billiards matches, thousands of pounds changing hands in the course of a week. The more raffish enjoyed patronising boxing matches, whose rules the Marquess of Queensbury had reformed, and could even watch boxing contests in the comfort of clubs like the Pelican that were devoted to sport and sportsmen.

LIFE ON THE GRAND SCALE

Rich Americans with 'old money' might live in a style very similar to that of the English gentry, but the New Rich, with annual incomes amounting to millions of dollars, could live in a truly spectacular manner. Andrew Carnegie had an average annual income between 1896 and 1900 of $10 million. He was modest in his personal tastes, but he lavished money on a castle and a 32 000 acre (13 000 ha) estate in Scotland. Other millionaires showed off their wealth by building themselves palatial houses.

The Vanderbilts led the way. By the mid-1880s they had no fewer than seven great houses on Fifth Avenue, New York, alone, costing a total of over $12 million and filled with costly furniture and works of art. Two of them were built in the style and on the scale of the great French chateaux of the Loire. For an escape

POT THAT By the 1900s, the aristocratic game of billiards was becoming familiar to the middle classes.

from the city they built even more massive houses, which they called cottages, such as Cornelius Vanderbilt's 'The Breakers' and William K. Vanderbilt's 'Marble House' in Newport, Rhode Island, and Frederick W. Vanderbilt's house at Hyde Park, with its 50 ft (15 m) dining room, and William K.'s Idle Hour on Long Island, with 110 rooms, 45 bathrooms and garaging for 100 automobiles.

Greatest of all was George W. Vanderbilt's 'Biltmore' at Asheville, North Carolina, with 40 master bedrooms, a Court of Palms, an Oak Drawing Room, a Banqueting Hall, a Tapestry Gallery and a Library containing 250 000 volumes. All in all, it was estimated at that time that the Vanderbilts had invested as much money in the erection of new buildings as any of the royal families of Europe, with the exception of the Bourbons.

In such houses, the new millionaires attempted to live the princely life, surrounded by marble staircases, tapestries, velvet and brocade, pipe organs, potted palms and classical statues holding electric light fixtures. One American journalist described Henry C. Frick, the steel millionaire, 'in his palace, seated on a Renaissance throne under a baldachino [ceremonial canopy], and holding in his little hand a copy of the *Saturday Evening Post*.' And another pointed out that whereas the European chateaux on which these houses were modelled had been public as well as private places, centres of local government and patronage, as private homes they were quite anomalous, even if they were provided not only with Renaissance paintings, Greek statuary and Flemish tapestries, but also with modern plumbing and heating

FAMILY SNAPSHOT A Tasmanian family enjoy a picnic in a park, at a picnic site much like those in public parks today, and have their photograph taken to commemorate the day.

own private Nile steamer. John D. Rockefeller also liked to live quietly despite a colossal fortune from oil revenues, but his estate near New York had 75 buildings, garages for 50 cars, and 70 miles (110 km) of private roads, and employed between 1000 and 1500 staff, according to the season.

systems, electric light, automatic elevators and internal telephone systems.

J. Pierpont Morgan disliked this kind of vulgar display, but he himself had a priceless collection of rare books and works of art, a country house at Highland Falls, a house in London and an English country house, a 1000 acre (405 ha) estate in the Adirondacks, a 'fishing box' at Newport, his own suites at the Hotel Bristol in Paris and the Grand Hotel in Rome, a 302 ft (92 m) steam yacht and his

SOCIETY ENTERTAINMENTS

English and French 'Society' was centred in London and Paris. American Society was dispersed among its larger cities, but New York Society was pre-eminent. In 1892, Ward McAllister, a Southerner who was regarded at the time as the arbiter of elegance, declared that even if Mrs Astor's ballroom held only 400 people it was big enough,

---

EYEWITNESS

THE HEIGHT OF THE SEASON

Mark Twain, visiting Australia on a lecture tour in 1895, was in no doubt that Melbourne Cup Day, inaugurated in 1861, was the nation's supreme social and sporting event.

❛ They come a hundred thousand strong, as all the best authorities say, and they pack the spacious grounds and grandstands and make a spectacle such as is never to be seen in Australasia elsewhere.

It is the "Melbourne Cup" that brings this multitude together. Their clothes have been ordered long ago, at unlimited cost, and without bounds as to beauty and magnificence, and have been kept in concealment until now, for unto this day are they consecrate. I am speaking of the ladies' clothes, but one might know that.

And so the grandstands make a brilliant and wonderful spectacle, a delirium of colour, a vision of beauty. The champagne flows, everyone is vivacious, excited, happy; everybody bets, and gloves and fortunes change hands right along, all the time. Day after day the races go on, and the fun and excitement are kept at white heat; and when each day is done, the people dance all night so as to be fresh for the race in the morning. And at the end of the great week the swarms secure lodgings and transportation for next year, then flock away to their remote homes and count their gains and losses, and order next year's Cup-clothes, and then lie down and sleep two weeks, and get up sorry that a whole year must be put in somehow or other before they can be wholly happy again. ❜

SIMPLE PLEASURES The humblest Englishmen could enjoy the pleasures of the beach, as here at Sheringham, Norfolk. The French (inset) delighted in the social life of the bar-cabaret.

since there were only about 400 people who counted. Hence the world of the Four Hundred, in which the New Rich strove to achieve recognition by acquiring splendid houses, elegant equipages and liveried servants and by entertaining on the most lavish scale, but also, they hoped, in the 'correct' manner.

In 1897 the Bradley Martins gave a ball estimated to cost $370 000. At Newport in 1902 the Vanderbilts gave an 'at home' on an estate borrowed from the Astors, which included such entertainments as shooting galleries, Negro dancers, singing girls, a *Punch and Judy* show, and the performance of a musical comedy transported from Broadway to a theatre specially erected on the estate for the occasion.

For another party, 'Mrs Belmont imported Chinese artisans to construct a red and gold lacquer teahouse on the cliffs at Marble House. The structure was gorgeous and authentic, but contained no provision for making tea. A miniature railroad was therefore laid from the pantry of the mansion to the cliffs, its course masked by elaborate planting, and footmen with trays were thereby whisked down to the lacquered toy.'

MAD TO TANGO

The tango was a controversial dance. In April 1914, the jury at a commission of lunacy in Savannah, Georgia, decided that a woman named Sadie Jefferson was not insane, despite her having danced the tango. It was alleged that after being arrested she had tangoed all the way to police headquarters.

Dinners in New York and Newport were commonly served for 100 or more guests, with eight or more courses and a wide variety of wines. When Randolph Guggenheimer gave a dinner for 40 at the Waldorf-Astoria in 1899 he had the room transformed into a garden, with roses, hyacinths and tulips in bloom, and nightingales, blackbirds and canaries singing in the foliage. More than 20 separate dishes were served, at a cost of $250 a head (perhaps $4000, or £2600, at today's values).

For those with social aspirations, the badge of success was to be invited to one of Mrs Astor's massive dinners. But there were those, still socially insecure, who sought the authentic stamp of aristocracy by marrying into the British or European nobility, as scores of American heiresses did in the 1890s and early 1900s. Most famous of all was the marriage of Consuelo Vanderbilt to the Duke of Marlborough. When money married title, there

was almost invariably a price. In the case of this marriage, it was 'the sum of two million five hundred thousand dollars in fifty thousand shares of the Beech Creek Railway Company', the income on which was to be payable to the Duke for his life.

TAKING THE PLUNGE   In the relaxed
spirit of the times, young New Yorkers
cool off in the Hudson River.

TIME CHART

WORLD EVENTS

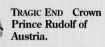

TRAGIC END Crown Prince Rudolf of Austria.

1887 Queen Victoria celebrates her Golden Jubilee.

1888 Wilhelm II becomes German Kaiser.

The Suez Canal is opened to ships of all nations.

1889 The Austrian Crown Prince Rudolf commits suicide at his hunting lodge at Mayerling.

General Boulanger fails to seize power in France.

The Dakotas, Montana and Washington become members of the United States.

Ethiopia becomes an Italian protectorate.

Cecil Rhodes founds the British South Africa Company.

1890 Kaiser Wilhelm II dismisses Bismarck as German Chancellor.

Idaho and Wyoming become members of the United States.

Cecil Rhodes becomes prime minister of Cape Colony.

The first general election is held in Japan.

EMPIRE-BUILDER Cecil Rhodes is instrumental in extending the British Empire in Africa.

ARTS AND LEISURE

1887 The first Celluloid film is developed by H.W. Goodwin.

1888 Vincent Van Gogh paints *The Yellow Chair,* one of a group of paintings that mark his first expressionist period.

George Eastman perfects the Kodak box camera.

The British Football League and the Lawn Tennis Association are founded.

1889 Gustave Eiffel designs the Eiffel Tower, 985 ft (300 m) in height, for the Paris Exhibition.

NEW ART Vincent Van Gogh's *The Yellow Chair.*

Football goal-nets are used for the first time in a match between Bolton Wanderers and Nottingham Forest.

BOOKS Sir Arthur Conan Doyle *A Study in Scarlet*, the first Sherlock Holmes story; Emile Zola *La Terre* (1887); Rudyard Kipling *Plain Tales from the Hills* (1888); Mark Twain *A Connecticut Yankee in King Arthur's Court* (1889).

THEATRE AND MUSIC Verdi's *Otello* (1887); Gilbert

and Sullivan *The Yeomen of the Guard* (1888); *The Gondoliers* (1889); Henrik Ibsen *Hedda Gabler* (1890); Tchaikovsky's opera *The Queen of Spades* (1890).

NEW HEIGHTS The Eiffel Tower remains the tallest building in the world for the next 40 years.

A CHANGING WORLD

1887 Edison and Swan combine to produce Ediswan light bulbs.

Paris and Brussels are the first cities to be linked by telephone.

The first-ever motor race is held on April 20 on a course between Saint-James in Paris and Neuilly. The one competitor drives a steam quadricycle.

1888 J.B. Dunlop invents the pneumatic tyre for his son's bicycle.

At least six women are murdered in London's East End by 'Jack the Ripper'.

MOTORING The daughters of Karl Benz in an early motor car.

Karl Benz sells the first petrol-driven motor car, a three-wheeled two-seater.

The first chewing-gum vending machines are installed in New York.

The first working-class dwellings to include bathrooms are built at Port Sunlight, Cheshire.

1889 The first jukebox, incorporating an Edison phonograph, is installed in San Francisco.

The first disc-playing gramophones are manufactured by Kammerer and Rheinhardt in Germany.

The first coin-operated telephone call-box is installed in Hartford, Connecticut.

1890 The Forth Railway Bridge is opened in Scotland.

The first entirely steel-framed building is erected in Chicago.

The first submarine telephone cable links France and England.

Old-age pensions are introduced in Germany.

WORLD EVENTS

France and Russia form an Entente.

The Young Turk movement, aimed at modernising Turkey, is formed in Geneva.

An earthquake in Japan kills around 10 000 people.

1892 William Gladstone becomes British prime minister for the fourth time.

Grover Cleveland is elected president of the USA.

Keir Hardie becomes the first British Labour MP.

1893 A Franco-Prussian Alliance is signed.

In Britain, the Independent Labour Party is formed.

1894 In France, Captain Alfred Dreyfus is arrested on treason charges.

Nicholas II becomes Tsar of Russia.

1895 Cuba starts a war of independence from Spain.

CAUSE CELEBRE Alfred Dreyfus is imprisoned on Devil's Island, French Guiana

RUINS The Japanese city of Ogaki is devastated by an earthquake.

1891 The Triple Alliance between Germany, Austria and Italy is renewed.

ARTS AND LEISURE

1891 The painter Paul Gaugin settles in Tahiti.

Motion pictures are demonstrated publicly for the first time at the Edison laboratories in West Orange, New York.

1892 'Gentleman Jim' Corbett defeats John L. Sullivan in 21 rounds and becomes world heavyweight boxing champion.

An exhibition in Berlin of strongly expressionistic paintings by Edvard Munch creates great controversy and closes after a week.

The Frenchman Louis Lumière invents the *cinématographe*. The first commercial showing of moving pictures takes place in New York.

URBAN ART Edvard Munch's *Spring Evening on Karl Johan Street*.

1895 The Art Nouveau style appears throughout Europe.

The British player Peter Latham becomes world lawn tennis champion.

The first US Open Golf Championship is held.

BOOKS Thomas Hardy *Tess of the D'Urbervilles* (1891); Oscar Wilde *The Picture of Dorian Gray* (1891); Zola *La Débâcle* (1892); Anthony Hope *The Prisoner of Zenda* (1894); Rudyard Kipling *The Jungle Book* (1894); H.G. Wells *The Time Machine* (1895).

THEATRE AND MUSIC
Gustav Mahler 1st Symphony (1891); Tchaikovsky's ballet *The Nutcracker* (1892); Dvorak's *Symphony No. 9* 'From the New World' (1893); Engelbert Humperdinck's opera *Hänsel und Gretel* (1893); Verdi's last great opera, *Falstaff* (1893); Oscar Wilde *The Importance of Being Earnest* (1895).

A CHANGING WORLD

1891 Construction of the Trans-Siberian Railroad begins in Russia.

Edward Prince of Wales appears as a witness in a libel action concerning allegations of cheating at cards.

Fingerprinting is used for the first time for identifying suspects, by the police in Buenos Aires.

Free state education is introduced in England. (It had been introduced in Scotland the previous year.)

The first electric oven produced for sale is manufactured in St Paul, Minnesota.

MEDICAL MILESTONE Roentgen's first X-ray photograph.

1892 The world's first escalator is installed, on Coney Island.

1893 Karl Benz builds his first four-wheel car and Henry Ford builds his first car.

Fridtjof Nansen begins his North Pole expedition.

The first vehicle registration plates are introduced in France.

1894 Coca-Cola is sold in bottles in the United States.

Death duties are introduced in Britain for the first time.

1895 Wilhelm Roentgen discovers X-rays.

The publication of Sigmund Freud's *Studies in Hysteria* marks the beginning of psychoanalysis.

Oscar Wilde brings his libel action against the Marquess of Queensbury, leading to his own trial, conviction and imprisonment.

FORERUNNER The earliest design for Coca-Cola bottles.

1896-1900

WORLD EVENTS

ALL AGES   Boer guerrilla fighters, aged (left to right) 65, 15 and 43.

1896 France annexes Madagascar.

1897 Queen Victoria celebrates her Diamond Jubilee.

1898 The United States declares war on Spain over Cuba and wins.

Empress Elizabeth of Austria is murdered by an Italian anarchist.

Zola publishes *J'accuse*, in support of Dreyfus, and is imprisoned.

William Gladstone, four times British prime minister, dies.

1899 The Boer War breaks out in Southern Africa.

Alfred Dreyfus is pardoned by presidential decree.

1900 The British

celebrate the relief of Ladysmith and Mafeking in South Africa.

The nationalist Boxer movement in China besieges foreign embassies in Peking and is only defeated through foreign intervention.

King Umberto of Italy is murdered by an anarchist and succeeded by his son, Victor Emmanuel III.

A Naval Law is introduced in Germany to increase the size of the navy, starting the armaments race with Britain.

60 GLORIOUS YEARS   A celebration mug for Queen Victoria's Jubilee.

ARTS AND LEISURE

1896 The Nobel prizes, for physics, physiology and medicine, chemistry, literature and peace, are established on the death of the Swedish industrialist Alfred Nobel.

The first modern Olympic Games, the inspiration of Baron de Coubertin, are held in Athens.

The first permanent cinema building opens, in New Orleans.

The Australian soprano Dame Nellie Melba appears at Covent Garden, London.

1897 The first comic strip appears, in the USA.

DIVA   The opera star Dame Nellie Melba.

1898 The first photographs to use artificial light are taken.

1899 Johann Strauss 'The Waltz King' dies.

1900 The 'Cake Walk' becomes a popular dance.

Oscar Wilde dies in disgrace in Paris.

The Davis Cup for lawn tennis is presented for the first time, to the US team.

Women compete for the first time in the Olympic Games.

BOOKS   Thomas Hardy's last novel, *Jude the Obscure* (1896); H.G. Wells *The Invisible Man* (1897); Henry James *The Turn*

MIND-DOCTOR Sigmund Freud developed comprehensive theories on the functioning of the human mind.

of the Screw (1898); H.G. Wells *The War of the Worlds* (1898); Joseph Conrad *Lord Jim* (1900)

THEATRE AND MUSIC   Puccini *La Bohème* (1896); Anton Chekhov *Uncle Vanya* (1897); Edward Elgar *The Enigma Variations* (1899); Puccini *Tosca* (1900).

A CHANGING WORLD

TAKING OFF   The Zeppelin airship, with a crew of five, lifts off for the first time.

1896 The Gold Rush to the Klondike, Canada, begins.

Guglielmo Marconi gives the first

public demonstration of wireless in London.

1897 The Royal Automobile Club is founded.

Ronald Ross discovers the malaria bacillus.

1898 The Paris Metro opens.

Pierre and Marie Curie discover radium and polonium.

Count Zeppelin builds his first airship.

King Leopold of Belgium becomes the first European monarch to own a motor car.

1899 The first radio distress signal

is transmitted by the East Goodwin lightship.

1900 Arthur Evans discovers the remains of Minoan civilisation in Crete.

Sigmund Freud's *The Interpretation of Dreams*, thought by many to be his greatest work, is published.

The distinctive Toblerone chocolate bar, the only chocolate mould ever to be patented, is imported into Britain.

UNIQUE   The patent for the Toblerone chocolate bar is signed by Albert Einstein.

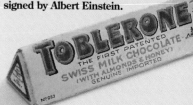

1901-1905

1901 Queen Victoria dies and is succeeded by King Edward VII.

US President McKinley, inaugurated for a second term in March, is assassinated in September.

Theodore Roosevelt becomes US President.

The Socialist Revolutionary Party is founded in Russia.

1902 The Boer War ends with the Peace of Vereeniging.

1903 The documents showing Dreyfus's guilt are proved to be forgeries.

1904 Britain and France sign the Entente Cordiale.

US engineers begin work on the Panama Canal.

1905 An attempted revolution in Russia is bloodily suppressed. Tsar Nicholas II promises reforms.

The Russian fleet is heavily defeated by the Japanese Navy at Tsushima.

Sailors of the Russian battleship *Potemkin* mutiny.

Norway declares independence from Sweden.

FIRST FAMILY   US President Theodore Roosevelt and his family in 1903.

The Sinn Fien Party is established in Dublin.

NEW STYLE   Poster for the Vienna Secession Exhibition of 1902.

1901 The first exhibition of Picasso's work is held in Paris.

Giuseppe Verdi dies; his operas spanned half a century.

1902 The Secessionist school of art and design in Vienna, which promotes the Art Nouveau style, holds its fourteenth exhibition.

Elgar composes the first of his 'Pomp and Circumstance' marches.

The film *The Great Train Robbery* is the longest to date (12 minutes).

FUNCTIONALISM   A Frank Lloyd Wright house in Chicago.

Frank Lloyd Wright designs his first 'prairie' house, establishing a new style of functional architecture.

1903 The first baseball World Series is won by the Boston Red Sox.

The first Tour de France bicycle race takes place.

The Abbey Theatre, Dublin, is founded.

BOOKS Thomas Mann *Buddenbrooks* (1901); Joseph Conrad *Heart of Darkness* (1902); Arthur Conan Doyle *The Hound of the Baskervilles* (1902); A.E.W. Mason *The Four Feathers* (1902); Jack London *Call of the Wild* (1903); Henry James *The Golden Bowl* (1904); Edith Wharton *The House of Mirth* (1905).

THEATRE AND MUSIC Rachmaninov Piano Concerto No. 2 (1901); Maxim Gorky *The Lower Depths* (1902); George Bernard Shaw *Man and Superman* (1903); first performance of J.M. Barrie's *Peter Pan* (1904); Puccini's *Madam Butterfly* (1905); Franz Lehar's *The Merry Widow* (1905).

1901 The Cadillac car company is formed in Detroit, Michigan.

The patent for the safety razor is filed by Gillette in the USA. The razors went on sale three years later.

Marconi makes his first transatlantic radio transmission.

Andrew Carnegie sells the Carnegie Steel Company to the US Steel Corporation for $447 000 000 and sets up the Carnegie Trust.

1902 The binding of women's feet is officially abolished in China.

Berlin's first underground railway is opened.

A new speed record for cars of 74 mph

GENIUS   Albert Einstein as a young man.

(120 km/h) is set in France.

1903 Wilbur and Orville Wright make the first successful powered flight.

Henry Ford founds his automobile company.

1904 Russian physiologist Ivan Pavlov trains dogs in experiments with conditioned reflexes.

The Trans-Siberian Railroad is completed.

Charles Rolls and Henry Royce combine to make cars.

The New York subway opens with a line between Broadway and City Hall.

1905 Albert Einstein publishes his Theory of Relativity.

REFLEX ACTION   In Pavlov's tests, a dog is conditioned to salivate at the sound of a bell.

1906-1910

WORLD EVENTS

AFTERMATH   San Francisco after the 1906 earthquake.

1906 San Francisco is devastated by an earthquake.

The first Parliament or Duma opens in St Petersburg.

1907 Ghandi begins a civil disobedience campaign in South Africa.

The world's most powerful warship, HMS *Dreadnought*, breaks records on her trials.

1908 The British Labour Party adopts socialism.

Herbert Asquith becomes British prime minister.

Austria formally annexes Bosnia and Herzegovina.

Crete declares union with Greece.

Pu Yi becomes Chinese emperor, aged two.

1909 William Taft is inaugurated as US President.

British Chancellor Lloyd George introduces his People's Budget.

Police arrest 120 British suffragettes outside the Houses of Parliament.

Commander Perry, US Navy, is the first person to reach the North Pole.

1910 The Union of South Africa is formed, with Louis Botha as its first prime minister.

Edward VII dies and is succeeded by George V.

ARTS AND LEISURE

1906 Upton Sinclair's *The Jungle* exposes scandals in the Chicago stockyards.

Picasso's painting *Les Demoiselles d'Avignon* heralds the birth of Cubism.

The first Ziegfeld Follies are staged in New York.

1908 Peter Behrens erects the first steel and glass building, the AEG Turbine building, in Berlin.

Jack Johnson is the first

CHAMPION   Jack Johnson, world champion boxer.

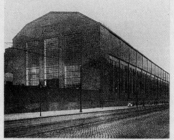

MODERNISM   The AEG Turbine building in Berlin.

black boxer to become world heavyweight champion.

1909 Nijinsky and Anna Pavlova lead the first season of Diaghilev's Ballets Russes.

1910 D.W. Griffith makes his first Hollywood film.

BOOKS John Galsworthy *The Man of Property* (1906); Joseph Conrad *The Secret Agent* (1907); E.M. Forster *A Room with a View* (1908); Kenneth Grahame *The Wind in the Willows* (1908); Arnold Bennett *The Old Wives' Tale* (1908).

THEATRE AND MUSIC
J.M. Synge's *The Playboy of the Western World* (1907); Gustav Mahler's 9th Symphony (1909); Stravinsky's ballet *The Firebird* (1910); Puccini *The Girl of the Golden West* (1910).

NEW DANCE   Isadora Duncan introduces a new style of dance.

A CHANGING WORLD

CHANNEL FLYER   Louis Blériot just before takeoff.

1906 The French Daracq racing car achieves a new land speed record of 108 mph (175 km/h).

'SOS' is adopted as the international wireless distress signal.

The Brazilian flyer Santos-Dumont makes a world-record flight of 235 yd (215 m).

The world's first holiday camp opens in Norfolk, England.

1907 London's music-hall artistes go on strike.

Robert Baden-Powell launches the Boy Scout movement.

The world's first women MPs are elected in Finland.

1908 In the USA, Buick and Oldsmobile combine to form General Motors.

The Model T Ford, the world's first mass-produced car, goes on sale.

1909 Selfridges department store opens in London.

The Pope beatifies Joan of Arc.

Louis Blériot makes the first cross-Channel flight.

Salvarson, Paul Ehrlich's antisyphillis drug, has its first successful trials in Frankfurt.

The word 'brassière' appears for the first time, in *Vogue* magazine.

1910 The Girl Scouts and the American Boy Scouts are founded.

Dr Crippen is charged with his wife's murder.

Elise Deroche is the first woman to be granted a pilot's licence.

1911–1914

1911 Winston Churchill is present as Home Secretary when police besiege anarchists in London's Sidney Street.

The Norwegian Roald Amundsen and his party are the first to reach the South Pole.

1913 Woodrow Wilson is inaugurated as US President.

DOOMED Archduke Franz Ferdinand of Austria shortly before his assassination.

The Ulster Unionists pledge themselves to resist Home Rule for Ireland.

The liner *Titanic* sinks in the North Atlantic on her maiden voyage.

1914 The Archduke Franz Ferdinand of Austria is assassinated by a Serb nationalist in Sarajevo. Austria-Hungary declares war on Serbia and the system of European alliances makes war inevitable.

Germany declares war on France and Russia and invades Belgium on August 4.

Britain declares war on Germany and sends troops to France.

1911 George Braque paints *Man with a Guitar*.

Leonardo's *Mona Lisa* is stolen from the Louvre.

The first Indianapolis 500 car race is held.

1912 Marcel Duchamp paints *Nude Descending a Staircase*.

Charles Pathé produces his first news film.

Contract bridge is played for the first time, in Poona, India.

BELLES LETTRES Marcel Proust, chronicler of *belle époque* society.

PUZZLER The first crossword is published in 1913.

1913 The 'Armory Show' introduces Cubism to New York.

Charlie Chaplin makes his film debut.

The foxtrot becomes fashionable.

1914 Charlie Chaplin stars in the film *Tillie's Puncture Romance*.

The tango, which had emerged in Argentina in the 1880s, becomes fashionable in Europe.

The Old Vic Shakespeare Company is founded in London.

BOOKS D.H. Lawrence *Sons and Lovers* (1913); Marcel Proust

publishes the first part of *A La Recherche du Temps Perdu* (1913); James Joyce *The Dubliners* (1914).

THEATRE AND MUSIC Irving Berlin 'Alexander's Ragtime Band' (1911); George Bernard Shaw *Pygmalion* (1912); Stravinsky *The Rite of Spring* (1913).

DIRTY DANCING The Argentinian tango becomes a scandalous sensation.

1911 The world's first white road markings are painted, in Michigan, USA.

The first official airmail flight takes place, in Allahabad, India.

1912 In the USA the Modesty League is formed to oppose tight dresses.

Carl Gustav Jung publishes his *Theory of Psychoanalysis*.

Motor ambulances are used for the first time at Tripoli during the Italo-Turkish War.

1913 The first ship passes through the Panama Canal.

In Britain a National Insurance Act provides for sickness benefits.

The *Aquitania*, the world's biggest liner, is launched in Scotland.

In London, the first Chelsea Flower Show is held.

In New York, Grand Central Station opens, along with the Woolworth Building, the world's tallest at that time.

1914 The first airline passenger service opens, in Tampa, Florida.

The first electric traffic lights are installed, in Cleveland, Ohio.

The first aeroplane to shoot down another is a French

Voisin, whose mechanic downs a German Aviatik with a machine-gun. Both the German pilots are killed.

SUMMER SEASON Edwardians visit the Royal Horticultural Society's Chelsea Flower Show.

INDEX

ACKNOWLEDGMENTS

Abbreviations:
T=Top; M=Middle; B=Bottom; R=Right; L=Left

BAL=Bridgeman Art Library, London
MEPL=Mary Evans Picture Library, London
V&A=Victoria & Albert Museum, London

1 Hulton Getty. **2-3** Brown Brothers. **4** Corbis-Bettman, TL; The Mansell Collection, TR; Hulton Getty, BR. **5** MEPL, TL, BR; Hulton Getty, TR, BL; Jean-Loup Charmet, MR. **6-7** *Cowes Regatta,* painting John Stickland Goodall, Christopher Wood Gallery, London/BAL. **7** Hulton Getty, TL; Culver Pictures Inc., TR. **8** Suddeutscher Verlag, T; Culver Pictures Inc., BR. **9** Jean-Loup Charmet, TL; MEPL, BR. **10** The Mansell Collection, TR; Edimedia, B. **11** MEPL, TL, BL; poster *Le Triomphe de l'Aviation,* BAL, TR. **12** *Coronation of Nicholas II,* painting Henri Gervex, Musée d'Orsay, Paris/Giraudon/BAL. **13** Hulton Getty, T; Jean-Loup Charmet, MR. **14** *The Marlborough Family,* painting John Singer Sargeant (Red Drawing Room, Blenheim Palace), Duke of Marlborough, TL; Hulton Getty, B. **15** MEPL, T, B. **16** *Journal et bouteille de vin,* collage, Juan Gris, Christie's, London/BAL, TL; *Unique Forms of Continuity in Space,* Umberto Boccioni, Mattioli Collection, Milan/BAL, TM; Hulton Getty, B. **17, 18** Hulton Getty. **19** Corbis-Bettman; MEPL, TR. **20** The Transport Museum, TL; Roger-Viollet, BL; MEPL, BR. **21** Ullstein Bilderdienst, TL; MEPL, BR. **22** MEPL, TR, MM, BL. **23** MEPL, TR, BL; Culver Pictures Inc., MR. **24** Roger-Viollet, TL; Branger-Viollet, BR. **25** Robert Opie Collection, TL; MEPL, MR. **26** MEPL, T, ML. **27** Jean-Loup Charmet, TR; Ullstein Bilderdienst, MM. **28** Arcaid/ Mark Fiennes, T; National Trust Photographic Library/Rupert Truman, MR; Jean-Loup Charmet, BL. **29** Arcaid/Richard Bryant. **30** Arcaid/Simon Mathews, T; *Earthenware Dish,* William de Morgan, V&A/BAL, ML; Bonhams/BAL, BR. **31** *The Straw Plaiters,* painting Carlton Alfred Smith, Luton Museum/BAL. **32** BAL, ML; Topham Picture Library, BL. **33** Jean-Loup Charmet, T; Hulton Getty, MR. **34** Hulton Getty. **35** Lever Bros. Ltd, Cheshire/BAL, TL; MEPL, TM, BR; Private Collection/BAL, TR. **36-37** Illustration by Christian Hook. **38** Bournville Archives, T; MEPL, ML. **39** Hulton Getty, TL; MEPL, MR; Private Collection/ BAL,BR. **40** *The Harvest,* painting Pierre-Georges Dieterre, Musée des Beaux-Arts, Rouen/BAL, T; Ullstein Bilderdienst, ML; The Rural History Centre, BR. **41** Ullstein Bilderdienst. **42** Spaarnestad Fotoarchief, T;

Hulton Getty, BR. **43** Jean-Loup Charmet, T; Hulton Getty, MR. **44** Arcaid/Richard Bryant. **45** Design Alphonse Mucha, 1902, V&A/BAL, T; MEPL, B. **46** MEPL, TR; Science & Society Picture Library, BL. **47** MEPL. **48** Arcaid/Lucinda Lambton, TL; MEPL, TR, BL. **49** MEPL. **50** *Bathroom in the Home of Mrs Helen Terry Potter, 1909,* photograph John Byron/Museum of the City of New York, TL; MEPL, MR. **51** Arcaid/Lucinda Lambton, TL; MEPL, BR. **52** MEPL, T, MM; Superstock, ML. **53** Robert Opie Collection, TL; National Trust Picture Library, TR; Jean-Loup Charmet, BR. **54** Corbis-Bettman, TM; MEPL, TR; Hulton Getty, BL. **55** MEPL. **56** New York State Historical Society, Cooperstown. **57** Hulton Getty. **58** Hulton Getty, TL; MEPL, BM. **59** Kodak Museum, TL; MEPL, TR, MM; Ullstein Bilderdienst, BR. **60** MEPL. **61** MEPL, TR. **62** Jean-Loup Charmet. **63** Popperfoto. **64** Ullstein Bilderdienst, TL; MEPL, TR, BL. **65** Hulton Getty. **66** Ullstein Bilderdienst. **67** Hulton Getty, TR; MEPL, B. **68** *The Poor Picking Coal in a Worked-out Pit, 1894,* painting Nikolaj Alexejewitsch Kassatkin, Novosti/BAL. **69** Roger-Viollet, BL; MEPL, BR. **70** New York State Historical Society, Cooperstown. **71** Ullstein Bilderdienst, TL; MEPL, MM. **72** Hulton Getty. **73** British Library/ BAL. **74-75** MEPL. **75** NSPCC Photographic Library, TL. **76** MEPL. **77** Hulton Getty, T; MEPL, MR. **78** Kodak Museum. **79** Special Collections Division, University of Washington Libraries, negative no: UN #1547. **80** Robert Opie Collection, TL; Ullstein Bilderdienst, BL; ©Frederik Warne, BR. **81** V&A. **82** Hulton Getty, T; The Salvation Army, BL. **83** Robert Opie Collection. **84** MEPL, TL, BR. **85** Hulton Getty. **87** The Walter Collection; MEPL, TR. **88** Roger-Viollet, T; Robert Opie Collection, BL. **89** MEPL, TR, BL. **90** Robert Opie Collection, TL, B. **91-92** Hulton Getty. **93** Suddeutscher Verlag, TL; MEPL, BR. **94** Maggie Murray/Format, TL; MEPL, TR. **95** MEPL, TL, BR. **96** MEPL. **97** MEPL, T, BL; Hulton Getty, MR. **98** MEPL, TL. **99** MEPL, TL; Trinity College, Cambridge, TR; Ullstein Bilderdienst, BR. **100** Hulton Getty; MEPL, BL. **101** Corbis-Bettman. **102** Hulton Getty, T, BL. **103** Hulton Getty. **104** Hulton Getty, TL; MEPL, TM. **105** Suddeutscher Verlag, TL; Hulton Getty, BL, BR. **106** Hulton Getty. **107** MEPL, TL, BR; Hulton Getty, T. **108** MEPL. **109** Topham Picture Library, TL; Corbis-Bettman, MR; Hulton Getty, BR. **110** MEPL, ML; Suffolk Photographic Survey, B. **111** MEPL. **112** Hulton Getty, TL; MEPL, TR, BR. **113** MEPL, TM; Hulton Getty, BR. **114** Hulton Getty. **115** David King Collection. **116** MEPL, TM, BL; Hulton

Getty, BM. **117** Hulton Getty. **118** Corbis-Bettman, BL. **119** Corbis-Bettman, T; MEPL, MR; Culver Pictures Inc., BR. **120** WH Smith Limited. **121** Hulton Getty; BAL, BR. **122-3** Illustration by Gill Tomblin. **124** The Kobal Collection, TL, TR, ML. **125** *The Auditorium of the Old Castle Theatre,* painting Gustav Klimt, Historisches Museum der Stadt, Vienna/BAL, T; Hulton Getty, BR. **126** Hulton Getty, TL; poster Alphonse Mucha, V&A/BAL, TR. **127** *Marcelle Lender Dancing the Bolero in Chilperie,* 1895 painting Henri Toulouse-Lautrec, Private Collection/BAL. **128** Hulton Getty, TL, ML; MEPL, BR. **129** *Nijinsky's Costume for L'Après Midi d'un Faune,* painting Leon Bakst, Bibliothèque Nationale, Paris/ BAL, TL; Mander & Mitchenson Theatre Collection, TM. **130-1** Hulton Getty. **131** Superstock, TL. **132** MEPL, TL. **133** Hulton Getty. **134** Marlborough Cricket Club, ML; MEPL, B. **135** Hulton Getty, T; MEPL, TR; V&A/BAL, BL. **136** Hulton Getty. **137** MEPL, TL, MR; Hulton Getty, B. **138** Hulton Getty, TR; MEPL, BL. **139** Hulton Getty, T, BR. **140** Suddeutscher Verlag, T; *Hunting Scene,* painting E.A.S. Douglas, Cadogan Gallery, London, ML. **141** Suddeutscher Verlag, TL; *Portrait of the Astor Family,* 1850, painting Lucius Rossi, Private Collection. **142** Hulton Getty, TR; MEPL, BR. **143** Roger-Viollet, T; Hulton Getty, MR. **144, 145** MEPL, TR, BL. **146** Archives Office of Tasmania. **147** Brown Brothers. **148** Roger-Viollet, TL. **148, 149** Hulton Getty. **149** Brown Brothers. **150** Suddeutscher Verlag, TL, BM; Hulton Getty, TR; *Vincent's Chair, 1888,* painting Vincent van Gogh, Tate Gallery, London/BAL, ML; Hulton Getty, MR; **151** Popperfoto, TL; MEPL, TR; *Spring Evening on Karl Johann Street, Oslo, 1892,* painting Edvard Munch, Rasmus Meyers Samlinger, Bergen/BAL, MM; Hulton Getty, BL; Robert Opie Collection, BR. **152** Hulton Getty, TL; Robert Opie Collection, BR; Popperfoto, ML, MR; Suddeutscher Verlag, BL. **153** Corbis-Bettman, TR; *Poster for the 14th Exhibition of Vienna Secession, 1902,* Alfred Roller, Private Collection/BAL, ML; Arcaid/ Barbara Godzikowska, MM; Hulton Getty, BM; Toucan Books Archive, BR. **154** Corbis-Bettman, TL; Popperfoto, ML; AEG Archive, Berlin, MM; Brown Brothers, MR; Hulton Getty, BL. **155** Hulton Getty, TL, MM, BR; Toucan Books Archive, ML.

Front cover: MEPL, TR, BL; BAL, ML; Jean-Loup Charmet, MR; Hulton Getty, BM, BR.

Back cover: Jean-Loup Charmet, TL, MR, BL; BAL, TR; Hulton Getty, MM; MEPL, BM, BR.

The publishers are grateful to the following individuals and publishers for their kind permission to quote passages from the publications below:

Jonathan Cape Ltd from *There Was a Time* by Walter Greenwood, 1967.
Carcanet Press Ltd from *Goodbye to All That* by Robert Graves, 1929.
David Higham Associates and Allen Lane, The Penguin Press from *Akenfield* by Robert Blythe, 1969.
Hutchinson from *Me* by Naomi Jacob, 1933.
Reed Books from *Drawn from Memory* by Ernest Shepard, Methuen, 1957.
Oxford University Press from *A London Home in the 1890's* by M.V. Hughes, 1937.

59-016-1